GROWING, SHARING, SERVING . . .
"This book is a helpful offering in a needed field. It is focused on the woman in ministry, particularly in the church, and urges the fulfillment of the biblical injunction of older women to teach younger women—a vital necessity today."

John MacArthur
Pastor
Community Church of the Valley

GROWING SHARING SERVING

JO BERRY

David C. Cook Publishing Co.
ELGIN, ILLINOIS—WESTON, ONTARIO

© 1979 David C. Cook Publishing Co.
All rights reserved. With the exception of specifically indicated material and brief excerpts for review purposes, no part of this book may be reproduced or used in any form without written permission from the publisher.

Scripture quotations, unless otherwise noted, are from the New American Standard Bible.

Edited by Sharrel Keyes
Cover design by Larry Taylor and Kurt Dietsch
Printed in the United States of America
ISBN 0-89191-073-5
LC 78-73461

First printing—March 1979
Second printing—April 1979

To all of the women who helped pioneer these ideas—especially Nancy, Irene, and the gals in my Bible study groups. And to John, for letting me try.

CONTENTS

	Preface	9
1	New Challenges for Today	11
2	Getting Started	21
3	The Concept of Women's Ministries	38
4	The Priscilla Principle	50
5	The Gifts God Has Given Us	61
6	The Positives in Negatives	70
7	Creative Instigation	81
8	Successful Strategies	96
9	Performance Standards	112
10	Person-to-Person Sharing	123
11	Challenges in Serving	135
12	Spiritual Dimensions	146

PREFACE

In 1966 God planted a seed in my thinking; He gave me a dream in two words: *women's ministries*. At first, when I mentioned the idea, people would look rather puzzled and say, "Women's what?"

Then, in the years that followed, as I studied, taught, and eventually was hired to work in children's and women's ministries on a church staff, that seed grew. I was excited to discover, as I dug into the Scriptures and asked women to implement what was there, that the Bible contains a fully detailed plan for what women should be doing with their lives, both in the world at large and in the church.

I know now that God planted similar seeds in the

hearts and minds of many women. He is, in this decade that has rightfully been labeled "the era of woman," bringing it to fruition. I am convinced that God has an answer to the questions and doubts raised in the minds of Christian women by the women's liberation movement and by their own determination to be actively involved in their homes, communities, and the world. That answer is found in the concept of women's ministries.

I want you to be stirred and excited about the myriad of possibilities that are open to you. I hope this book will help you decide how you can serve effectively in your home, community, place of employment, and church: to do a dream!

NEW CHALLENGES FOR TODAY
1

TODAY'S WOMAN FACES many new challenges breaking down stereotypical barriers and opening new doors. The simple life in which roles were clearly delineated is gone, and in its place is a complex network of choices.

What excites me most about the present era is that, with a little ingenuity and thoughtfulness, a woman no longer needs to be put in a box with a singular title on it. The Christian woman can openly effect godly changes in her home, community, and church without the fear of being labeled a fanatic. She can openly express her faith and beliefs and implement them as part of her philosophy of life.

Why is it, then, that many Christian women seem to be

GROWING, SHARING, SERVING

pulling back from these new challenges rather than using them to their advantage? Why aren't we speaking up, as do the liberals and worldly activists? I think there are two major reasons: complacency and spiritual sterility.

Look up the word *complacent* in a dictionary. Write the definition here.

_____

_____

Now read Isaiah 32: 9-11 in a modern translation. How does God describe complacency in this passage?

_____

_____

ARE YOU A COMPLACENT DAUGHTER?

During the time of the prophet Isaiah, the women of Jerusalem were faced with a situation similar to the one we face today. There was political turmoil, and their society was in a state of decay. These women were unresponsive to the problems. They were pseudoinvolved in a few activities, but their lives were not having any effect.

Through His prophet, God gave these women the frightening warning you just read, one that can just as appropriately apply to us: "Rise up, you women who are at ease, and hear my voice; give ear to my word you complacent daughters. Within a year and a few days, you will be troubled O complacent daughters; for the vintage has ended, and the fruit gathering will not come. Tremble, you women who are at ease; be troubled, you complacent daughters" (Isa. 32: 9-11).

God warns us not to be at ease. *At ease* is a military

New Challenges for Today

term. We are challenged to come to attention. We are to be soldiers who are standing guard, taking note of what's happening and what our course of action should be, listening to what the Lord wants us to do.

The term *complacent daughters* is used three times in these three verses. What is complacency, and why is it so detrimental in the lives of God's women? Complacency has many facets. It is being satisfied with the status quo. It is not caring enough to be concerned; being unaffected by circumstances, events, or the plight of those less fortunate. It is being comfortably settled into the easy chair of our existence, with our feet propped up and our brains in neutral. It is detrimental because it results in inactivity and evokes no responses. Complacency is mental, physical, and spiritual detachment.

If we are complacent, we'll reach a point at which we quit producing altogether. Our adversary the devil never stops sowing; and when we do we give him ground to till and souls to harvest, he wins by default through our lack of effort.

God takes a very dim view of complacency. He says if we suffer from that condition, we should tremble and be troubled. We should be so frightened by what can happen that we should literally shake with fear. And internally we should be troubled, stirred up like a stormy sea. Christian women should be the spiritual and moral activists in their society, not complacent followers. Complacency can be conquered with just a little effort.

List three areas of your life in which you are suffering from complacency. Is it in your attitude toward your home? Do you pray consistently for the spiritual and physical welfare of your husband and children? Is it that you do things with a halfhearted attitude? Are you nega-

GROWING, SHARING, SERVING

tive about what is happening rather than positive about what you could be doing?

1. _____
2. _____
3. _____

Now list some areas in which you would like to become more active. Then write one commitment sentence telling what you will do to change yourself in these areas.

_____
_____

SPIRITUAL STERILITY

Why do so many Christian women stay out of causes, suffer from complacency, and become impotent in their faith? Why do they huddle cozily in the womb of their Christianity? One reason is a misunderstanding about what their approach to the world should be. They don't understand that Christ's prayer and desire for us is not opposed to our having contact with this wicked world but only to our conforming to it!

In the priestly prayer He uttered immediately before His betrayal and arrest, our Lord petitioned the Father with these words, "I do not ask Thee to take them out of the world, but to keep them from the evil one. . . . As Thou didst send Me into the world, I also have sent them into the world. And for their sakes I sanctify Myself, that they also may be sanctified in truth" (John 17:15, 18-19). So we are both sent and sanctified. We must not drag our heels in resistance!

New Challenges for Today

Another reason the Christian woman hesitates to become more involved is fear. It isn't easy to be *in* the world but not *of* it. Sin entices. We fall and flounder when we are faced with temptation. Since we cannot avoid the challenge of being in the world, we need to learn how to maintain our Christianity while we're in it. We do that by establishing a proper perspective about our position. Scripture tells us that our citizenship is in heaven and instructs us to "set your mind on the things above, not on the things that are on earth" (Col. 3:2). The principle we see here is that when our hearts are in the right place, it doesn't matter where our bodies are.

So, to settle comfortably into Christian circles is not biblical; it is selfish. We have the most precious commodity in the world—a knowledge of Christ—and we have the ability to perform a godly life in an ungodly world. Besides, there are advantages to increasing the sphere of our faith.

First, being in the world helps us keep the joy of our salvation. When do we get most excited about our Christianity? Is it when we hear a great sermon, or have a productive mission board meeting, or when we're typing postcards to help the church secretary? Probably not. Most likely it is when we see God working through us; when we share the gospel message or words of counsel from His Word and see lives changed for eternity. Sharing our faith with an unbelieving world keeps it new and fresh in our own lives.

Also, walking in the world helps us do things out of love rather than out of duty. When we get locked into a church ministry or settled comfortably behind the four walls of our own homes, pretty soon we start doing things because we have to or because we're pressured by the position rather than out of love for the Lord and concern for the people involved.

15

GROWING, SHARING, SERVING

I saw this happen in my own life when I was employed as a member of a church staff. I taught and administered; but after a while I wasn't doing it because I loved the Lord and wanted to serve Him, disciple His people, and share my faith but because it was a job requirement. I started to stagnate.

I remember that when I realized what my attitude was, I prayed and literally begged God to send me some kind of nonchurch-related ministry so I could regain the zeal I'd had when I was out in the world hammering out my theology. He responded the next day by giving me an outside teaching assignment in a women's organization whose main emphasis is evangelism.

The world is where fruit is produced. The orchard, the crop that Christ said is "white for harvest," is not in a church building. The majority of unbelievers are in the office where we work and in the houses on our blocks, not in our churches. Christ said we were chosen by Him to bear remaining fruit; we cannot neglect the field He has set before us.

Are you suffering from spiritual stagnation? Are you locked into people and positions rather than exploring the possibilities God has set before you?

Write in your own words a definition of *sterile*.

_____
_____
_____

Do you see any of your own traits in either the definition or the description? _____ yes _____ no
If yes, what specifically?

_____

THE STRATEGY

So what are some practical ways we can be in the world and not of it? How can we expand our horizons to meet the challenges God has offered in such abundance?

- *Have non-Christian friends.* Recently I met the dean of women at a Christian college. As we talked at lunch, I could tell this young woman was well informed about world affairs and local political and social issues. She was dressed impeccably and fashionably, yet modestly. When the conversation turned to the topic of leisure activities, she told me she played tennis regularly with several friends who aren't Christians. Her reason? She knew she'd "die on the vine" if she spent all of her time with people who believe as she does.

That's a wise lady. She knew how to be friends with someone without having close or permanent ties. Fellowship with other believers is sweet, but to win souls to Christ the Christian has to be with the lost and establish a witness through example.

- *Join non-Christian organizations.* Some Christians think all of a woman's talents and giftedness should be used in ministering within the local church. Maybe, in the keenest sense, we can't use our spiritual gifts in a political campaign or the PTA, but adding believers to the Body of Christ also edifies the church. Stating Christian principles to a non-Christian world will glorify God and counter unrighteous ideas with spiritual ones. Belonging to a secular organization gives us a platform from which to speak.

- *Learn about non-Christian things.* If we don't know what "they" believe, how can we comment on or counter their ideas intelligently? Christian women need to be up-to-date on issues so we can argue or defend from fact

GROWING, SHARING, SERVING

rather than emotion. "The Bible says" does not matter to someone who doesn't believe in it. We can start by reading the daily newspaper. (Even the sports page can be used to the Lord's advantage. I witnessed to our barber because I was up on the latest pro football news.) Write sponsoring organizations and government officials to get information about the plans and programs they support. Don't be an intellectual ostrich.

- *Exercise faith.* We aren't supposed to test God, but we are certainly supposed to use Him. It's one thing to believe something and quite another to put our faith into action in front of a bunch of skeptics. One of the greatest thrills in life is seeing God do in the midst of an unbelieving world what He's promised He'll do.

Many challenges beckon today's women. Are we ready to meet them? Will we forsake the complacency, sacrifice the comforts of our spiritual sterility, emerge victorious from the womb of our Christianity, and choose to face our God-given opportunities with a heart full of expectation and joy? Will we accept our Lord's challenge to be ministering women, to "rise up, you women who are at ease"?

WORKSHOP

What does each of these verses tell you to do? Your completed list will be a picture of a Christian activist.

James 1:22 _____

_____

1 John 4:7 _____

_____

New Challenges for Today

1 Peter 4:10 _____

Hebrews 13:2 _____

2 Timothy 2:15 _____

1 Thessalonians 5:17 _____

Philippians 4:6-8 _____

Ephesians 5:18 _____

Ephesians 4:32 _____

Galatians 6:2 _____

1 Corinthians 15:58 _____

Proverbs 31:27 _____

Now, let's test your spiritual sterility quotient.

1. I purposely cultivate non-Christian friends so I can witness and have a spiritual effect on their lives. _____ yes _____ no

2. I belong to at least one non-Christian organization. _____ yes _____ no

3. I am well versed on the issues facing the church and society today. _____ yes _____ no

4. I can carry on an informed and intelligent conversa-

GROWING, SHARING, SERVING

tion about politics and social issues and can defend my stands from an intellectual, reasonable point of view as well as from a spiritual one. _____ yes _____ no

5. I am bold about Christ and about my faith and speak up to defend the Christian position when I am in a group. _____ yes _____ no

GETTING STARTED
2

EACH OF US WANTS to do more than we're doing, to minister more fully and effectively. This chapter is a checklist of basic concepts that will help us evaluate our positions and lay the groundwork for developing and expanding our ministries.

1. MOTIVATION: WE ARE CALLED

In John 17:18 Christ says, "As Thou didst send Me into the world, I also have sent them into the world." We are to represent Christ.

GROWING, SHARING, SERVING

When I eat at a new restaurant and am impressed by the food and service, I tell my friends and business associates about it. When I find a bargain in a store, I call my friends so they can get in on the deal. I am motivated by what I find that is of benefit to me, and I want to pass it on to others. How much more so with Christ!

In the space below, list as many reasons as you can for dedicating yourself to serving the Lord by being creatively involved in your home, community, and church.

_____
_____
_____

2. PURPOSE: TO SHARE THE ABUNDANT LIFE

Christ promised His sheep (those who follow Him) an abundant life. "I came that they might have life, and might have it abundantly" (John 10:10). God wants to use us in discerning and meeting the needs of others. Everyone we know and love could be living an abundant life with Christ. But are they?

As we look around and see the lostness and misery in people's lives, we are also viewing our purpose: to minister to the multitude of those people's needs. Those without Christ need to know Him and experience His abundance. Those who have taken the initial step of faith need to grow and learn how to live the abiding life.

Care, encouragement, and concern are almost lost commodities in today's world. In Christ we have so

Getting Started

much; we need to let our cups overflow onto others. Let's think through some ways to splash some of our godliness over onto others. Remember, these do not have to be monumental problems; just simple needs.

Who do you know who has a deep personal need?
_____

How can you help them? Set a definite time when you plan to do this.
_____
_____
_____

What is one need in your church? If you are not aware of any, call and ask if there is something you can do to be of help in some way.
_____
_____

What is one need in your home; what have you neglected doing, or what family member needs assistance in some way? How and when will you minister to this need?
_____
_____
_____
_____

Who are three people you should be praying for?
_____
_____
_____

Make a commitment to pray for them daily for one month.

GROWING, SHARING, SERVING

3. MISSION: COMMITMENT TO CHRIST

Just this morning my eight-year-old son, Brian, was singing as he was getting ready for school: "Be a missionary every day. Tell the world that Jesus is the way." He understands that he is a missionary, that God has given him a mission to do every day. Many Christians bog down before they ever get started, because they don't understand that they do have a mission, a definite one.

It is one thing to have a broad, general purpose to be a good Christian, to be obedient and to study; but it is quite another thing to implement our lives toward specific goals. To properly fulfill our mission, we need to determine one specific, practical area that can be a starting point for our growth.

In Matthew 4:19 Christ challenged His disciples to "follow Me." Then He promised, "And I will make you fishers of men." Three things stand out in that little verse about our mission. One, it is Christ we follow. Two, if we follow Him (and we do have a choice), He automatically enables us. He said, "*I* will make you." Three, our mission is to be a fisher for the souls of men.

So, to start your mission, look at the fishing ground where you are. Are you in a home with an unsaved husband or other family member? Are you in touch with Christians who need your constant loving encouragement? Are you in a neighborhood with people who may have never heard the claims of Christ or who have some very wrong opinions about Christianity because of some past experiences? Are you in some organization, such as the PTA, Little League board, or a women's club? Do you hold a job in an office, store, school, hospital, or industry? Think about your immediate environment, and

Getting Started

make a written commitment of some ways you can start working in your mission field.

_____

_____

_____

Commitment is the key to success in anything we do. I once had the privilege of watching a wise man choose a new employee for an executive position on his staff. He interviewed several capable and well-trained people. Then, looking over the applications, he pulled the name of someone I thought was one of the least qualified. That applicant didn't have as much education and experience and had seemed a bit unsure about the answers to a couple of the interview questions.

"This is definitely the man for the job," my friend said. When I asked him why he picked that man, he said something I've never forgotten. "He may lack experience, but he can learn the ropes and procedures easily enough. I chose him because he had something none of the others had. He was committed. It was obvious he wanted the job so badly that he would give it all he had. Commitment like that compensates for a lot of technical lacks."

4. THE SURETY: GOD'S PROMISES

No one likes to fail, and no one purposely tries to do something they know will not succeed. When we commit ourselves to the concept of Christian service, we have an ironclad guarantee from God that we will be effective. 1 Corinthians 15:58 says, "Be steadfast, immovable, al-

GROWING, SHARING, SERVING

ways abounding in the work of the Lord, knowing that your toil is not in vain in the Lord."

Nothing we do in the Lord is ever wasted or fruitless! There is not one thing we can do in life about which we can be 100 percent sure of the outcome, except in service to the Lord.

Why are so many Christians fearful? Why do they hesitate and feel so uncertain about doing the Lord's work? I think it may be because they forget that the results are His. They try to take over the role of the Holy Spirit and decide what should happen and how, rather than simply following Christ. They go their own way instead of taking God's lead.

Our attitude should be like that of a witness in court. A witness is called to testify about what he or she knows, not to make judgments or to convict. A witness who tried to usurp the role of the judge or jury would be thrown out of court.

In the same way, it is not the duty of the Christian to make judgments or to convict people concerning Christ. Our job is to labor for Him and testify as to what we know to be true about Him, both by word and example. When we do that, we can be certain the results will be what God wants.

Find dictionary definitions for the following words:

Steadfast _____

Immovable _____

Abounding _____

Work _____

Labor _____

Vain _____

Now write 1 Corinthians 15:58, using your new defini-

Getting Started

tions and putting your name in where the word *your* is used.

_____
_____
_____

5. THE POWER: DIVINE PROVISION

It is a lofty thing to be called to serve God! It is natural to wonder if you can possibly have the capacity to do it. 2 Peter 1:3 tells us that "His divine power has granted to us everything pertaining to life and godliness." That sentence assures us that we already have power, not some conjured-up human resource, but God's divine power. We have His supernatural energy available to us.

Since the power is from God, it is total, complete, and sufficient in every sense. We have the power to do anything God calls us to do; our efforts will be enabled by this reservoir of strength.

Now, look up the following verses, and write a sentence describing what each says about the power you can appropriate in your life.

Isaiah 40:29 _____

Acts 1:8 _____

Ephesians 1:19-20 _____

2 Timothy 1:7 _____

Ephesians 3:20 _____

List one thing you think God has wanted you to do that

you have not done. Do you have the strength to do it now?

6. THE PLACE: WHERE YOU ARE

For some reason, many Christians fear that if they make themselves available to God in the fullest sense, the first thing He will do is send them somewhere they do not want to go and make them do something they don't want to do. This satanic lie has caused vast numbers of God's people to hold back from total dedication to service. Acts 1:8 says, "You shall receive power when the Holy Spirit has come upon you; and you shall be My witnesses both in Jerusalem, and in all Judea and Samaria, and even to the remotest part of the earth."

Where should you begin? Do you have to go to Alaska or Africa? No! Your starting point, according to this verse, is anywhere you are. You begin your ministry in your Jerusalem.

Let me share from my experience. My Jerusalem is Granada Hills, California. I started by sharing with neighbors, grocery clerks, my hairdresser, my colleagues on the school faculty, and the parents of the boys in my son's Little League.

But it doesn't end there. As you serve in your Jerusalem, God expands your horizon to Judea and Samaria. The people you share with in your Jerusalem go out and they are, in effect, part of your ministry. Or, you can write letters to relatives in other parts of the country

Getting Started

and share Christian tapes and books. As you travel on business or vacations, you can plant seeds. Some of the most effective witnessing I have ever done has been on airplanes or in waiting rooms.

When we come to the part about the remotest part of the earth, you may not want to venture any further than the Caribbean or the Hawaiian Islands, and then only for a short time. I do not know how God will use you to minister far away, but I do know He will, and He will probably do it without changing your location.

In my case, He has done it through tapes I make and the books I write. I am still living in Granada Hills, California, but I am ministering to missionaries in Japan, to pastors' wives in South Africa, to a newly formed church in Honolulu, and to a small congregation in Alaska. All I did was serve where I am, and God moved my ministry into the remotest parts. He will do the same for you.

What are at least three ways you can minister in your Jerusalem?

_____

_____

What are at least three ways you can minister in your Judea and Samaria?

_____

_____

How can you begin?

_____

_____

GROWING, SHARING, SERVING

7. THE APPROACH: PRAY AND DO

God knows what He wants you to do to actually start your ministry, so the first thing you should do is the thing many of us usually do last: pray. Ask the One who is sending you what He has planned for you.

John 15:16 is one of the most exciting verses in the Bible. Jesus tells His disciples, "You did not choose Me, but I chose you, and appointed you, that you should go and bear fruit, and that your fruit should remain; that whatever you ask of the Father in My name, He may give to you." Base your approach to a new ministry, or a refreshment of your present one, on that verse. Pray that you will become an effective fruitbearer. Pray for the ones who will become part of your crop of fruit. Pray with others, so that they will see the power of God as He answers prayers for them.

Realize that Jesus Christ chose and appointed you for the very specific reason of going and bearing fruit for Him. The fruit you were chosen to bear is an exceptional kind. Christ called it, "remaining fruit." Unlike any other, this crop never dies, and it cannot be consumed or destroyed by the elements. Anytime you pray for fruit, God will answer abundantly, because it is His will that you bear fruit!

For several years I have used John 15:16 as a basis for prayer. As an example of how God has responded, I want to tell you about the dinner last night at the home of my friend Irene. Irene is being greatly used by the Lord to set up and structure discipleship courses for women in various churches. I listened to eight women tell how Irene's instruction and ministry in their lives had transformed them from spiritual wallflowers into dynamic disciplers.

Getting Started

Not all of the women Irene had discipled were there. Some of them have moved on to other states. One is in New York, another in Oregon, and Penny is moving to Arizona in two weeks. Each of them has started a discipleship ministry by which hundreds of women in the Christian community are being positively affected.

How do I fit into all of this? Seven years ago God dropped Irene in my lap and gave me the privilege of discipling her. We studied together weekly, prayed, and shared one another's burdens. Irene is part of my crop of remaining fruit, and I feel in my heart that every woman she helps has become a part of the remaining fruit Christ promised when I prayed.

Is your approach to life and ministry based on prayer? Write down several ways you want to be used to bear fruit, and commit these things to God daily; then watch the results!

_____

_____

_____

8. THE ATTITUDE: INFECTIOUS ENTHUSIASM

Someone once said, "Attitudes are infectious; are yours worth catching?" Not too long ago I joined a local gym. The membership fee was low, and both the facility and individual weight and exercise programs are outstanding. In a short time I lost not only pounds but inches. I have been so enthusiastic about the place that six of my friends also joined. They were infected by my enthusiasm.

GROWING, SHARING, SERVING

God wants you to have a <u>zealous attitude</u> about Him. <u>You will never be effective if you aren't excited about what you are doing.</u> The Lord takes a dim view of lukewarm Christians; He says, "I know your deeds, that they are neither cold nor hot; I would that you were cold or hot. So because you are lukewarm, and neither hot nor cold, I will spit you out of My mouth" (Rev. 3:15-16).

Have you ever thought about how unappealing lukewarm is? When you are tired, you do not want to take a lukewarm bath to relax. Or, when you are very thirsty, you don't want a glass of lukewarm water. You do not order a lukewarm pizza for dinner or crave a cup of lukewarm coffee first thing in the morning. Lukewarm, halfhearted attitudes are just as unappealing.

Look up the word *enthusiastic* in a dictionary and write at least six synonyms for it.

1. _____ 4. _____
2. _____ 5. _____
3. _____ 6. _____

Now, write four words that mean the opposite of *enthusiastic*.

1. _____ 3. _____
2. _____ 4. _____

Mark any words on either list that describe your attitude. Are you an enthusiastic witness for the Lord?

9. THE CREDENTIALS: THE WORD AND THE WAY

Women equip themselves for secular jobs through study and training. We should equip ourselves to serve the Lord, too. 2 Timothy 2:15 says, "Be diligent to pre-

Getting Started

sent yourself approved to God as a workman who does not need to be ashamed, handling accurately the word of truth."

Recently I helped organize a retreat. Rather than have one person teach most of the time, we decided to have study groups with leaders directing the discussion. Each leader was given a study sheet to prepare so she could present it to her group. One leader told me she had more fun doing her worksheet than she has had in a long time. Another said she did not realize what a little bit of time she had been devoting to formal Bible study. Still another confessed that being forced to prepare the materials had pointed out her own lack of study.

I'm afraid this is the case with many women who faithfully attend church, Bible studies, women's missionary organizations, and prayer meetings. Too many of us want to equip ourselves by osmosis rather than through diligent study. To be a minister of the Word, we must be students of it.

There is more to study than most people realize. I like to think of study as having three parts. The first is *devotions*, the emotional, communication part of study; the time when we pray, seek inspiration, and listen to the Lord. It is the silent closet time when God penetrates our consciences and spirits. I liken it to the sexual relationship in a marriage. It is the deeply personal time we spend in private, closed quarters with our Lord.

Another part of study is *Bible reading*. Some of you have probably attempted to read through the Bible, but if you are like me, you get as far as Genesis 5 and lose interest. I have found it is helpful if I pick a book and read it every day for a minimum of fifteen days. If the book is short, I might combine it with part of another. Or, if it is a long one, I may divide it into sections. But by reading daily, at the end of fifteen days, I know the book.

GROWING, SHARING, SERVING

It is also good to be reading through the Gospels at the rate of a chapter or two a day because they keep Christ in the foreground of your mind. If your pastor or Bible teacher is teaching from a particular book, you may want to read it.

A third activity is the part we usually think of when we use the word *study*, or choosing a passage of Scripture and working through it in detail. There are many ways to do this, but here is one I have found to be beneficial.

MATERIALS YOU WILL NEED: A King James Bible and at least one modern translation (NASB, RSV, or NIV)
A concordance
A topical Bible
A Bible dictionary
Underliner, pen, pencil, eraser, notepaper

GO TO: A comfortable place where you can spread out your materials and be undisturbed by room traffic, telephones, etc.

GET QUIET: Remove distractions.

PRAY: For wisdom, to be taught by the Spirit, to have your instruction sealed (Col. 1:9-12) (1 John 2:27)

READ: One of the Psalms or one of your favorite passages just to prepare your heart.

EXPECT: A reaction as you study. God deals with you through His Word if you're serious about your approach (Heb. 4:12).

GO TO: The passage you intend to study, or the lesson. Read it, and reread it in more than one translation as many times as you feel is necessary to really grasp the basic meaning.

Getting Started

THEN: Look for a principle in the passage, some overall truth that you can apply and use in a practical way.

NOW: Do a verse-by-verse, word-by-word study:
- Read a verse
- Underline the important ideas and words
- Check key words in your concordance and dictionary to get the exact meaning
- Look up related passages in your topical Bible.

Are you a student of the Word whom God would label a diligent workman? Fill in the blanks to see what your workmanship quotient is.

I presently spend _____ minutes a day in prayer and personal devotions.

I would like to spend _____ minutes a day in prayer and personal devotions.

The best time in my schedule to do this would be _____ . (I know one woman who has devotions in the shower, another when she eats breakfast, another when she is driving to work.)

I presently spend _____ minutes a day reading the Bible.

I would like to spend _____ minutes a day reading the Bible.

The best time for me to do this would be _____ .

I presently spend _____ minutes a day studying the Bible.

I would like to spend _____ minutes a day studying the Bible.

The best time in my schedule to do this would be _____ . (One television program missed equals

GROWING, SHARING, SERVING

one-half to one hour of study time every day.)

Total number of hours I presently spend daily in the three phases of study. ─────── Total number I plan to attain. ───────

10. THE RESULT: EXPANDED HORIZONS

There is no way any human mind could conceive of all the blessings God will send your way, but you can definitely expect your faith to be duplicated. When you share God's goodness and greatness with someone, they in turn share it with someone else, who also shares it. Your faith becomes known through theirs. And God uses you to produce remaining fruit, results that count for eternity.

In Romans 1:8 Paul says, "I thank my God through Jesus Christ for you all, because your faith is being proclaimed throughout the whole world." If your faith is in operation, that is what you can expect—that it will be proclaimed throughout the whole world! There is only one question left. Are you willing to do what is required to expand your horizons?

WORKSHOP

What do each of the following verses say to you personally?

Your motivation—John 15:13-14 ───────────

Getting Started

Your purpose—John 14:12 _____

_____

Your mission—Matthew 28:18-20 _____

_____

Your surety—Philippians 4:13 _____

_____

Your power—John 15:7-8 _____

_____

Your place—John 17:18 _____

_____

Your approach—Ephesians 5:18-19 _____

_____

Your attitude—Romans 12:11 _____

_____

Your credentials—2 Corinthians 5:20 _____

_____

The results—2 Peter 3:18 _____

_____

THE CONCEPT OF WOMEN'S MINISTRIES
3

I'LL NEVER FORGET THE DAY the Lord introduced me to the concept of women's ministries. I was studying specific Scriptures that pertain to women, and for the first time I read Titus 2:3-5. "Older women . . . are to be reverent in their behavior, not malicious gossips, nor enslaved to much wine, teaching what is good, that they may encourage the young women to love their husbands, to love their children, to be sensible, pure, workers at home, kind, being subject to their own husbands, that the word of God may not be dishonored."

I was both delighted and shaken. How could I have overlooked this passage for so long? Why had I never noticed it before? The impact of the content of those few

The Concept of Women's Ministries

words left me breathless. Here was a formula from God outlining how His women are to minister in His Body. I dissected and digested the verses with great glee.

PHILOSOPHY OF WOMEN'S MINISTRIES

This passage in Titus contains a wealth of information. It outlines the qualifications for women who want to be involved in a women's ministry and describes what its purposes are. It establishes the philosophy and lays the groundwork for such a ministry.

What is that basic philosophy? And why have God's women been so complacent toward it? I fear we've concentrated for so long on what we *can't* do that we've lost sight of what we *should* be doing. This has caused Christian women, in frustration, to seek and sometimes covet positions in the church that the Lord has specifically designed for men. As one woman told me, "I knew I should and could be doing a lot more than teaching Sunday school or going to a monthly missionary meeting, but no one ever told me what or how."

In most churches the congregation has been segregated into groups, supposedly to meet needs. Although some categorizing is necessary, to a great extent it has thwarted the basic purpose God extends to us in the second chapter of Titus. In this older-woman, younger-woman implementation, the ministry of the women within a church must overlap age and occupation barriers if it is to be successful. Singles and married women, homemakers and those employed outside the home, elderly and youthful, all minister to and with one another.

GROWING, SHARING, SERVING

I have found, as I speak to women's groups, that one of the most frequently stated needs is that single and young married women deeply desire an opportunity to spend quality social and spiritual time with older Christian women. Also, there are numerous junior-high and high-school girls who would greatly benefit from being friends with and being counseled by single girls who are a few years older than they. This can't be accomplished if sisters in Christ are consistently divided into age-graded, need-centered groups such as single mothers, weeping widows, or frivolous forties.

The basic philosophy of a women's ministry is that of overlapping services. A women's ministry is not a program but a way to create opportunities for women of all ages and status to use their gifts and talents to uplift one another. It's an attitude nurtured within individual women of serving and helping one another. It's instigating whatever must be done, as needs arise, to build women into fulfilled, responsible, active Christians who live out the concepts of Scripture in their everyday lives.

AN OLDER WOMAN

What are the qualifications for involvement in a women's ministry? Titus 2:3 includes both older women and younger women, so in some way that's all of us. The word *older* means "aged," advanced in years or experience, either in a physical or spiritual sense. These verses are a specific charge to older women, who are more spiritually mature in an area or responsibility. The Scripture in no way prohibits younger women from also teaching, sharing, and leading. The real beauty in this structuring is that no matter how young or old a woman is, there is always someone who is younger or older than she is. All women can and should minister and be ministered to.

SPIRITUAL STAIRSTEPPING

Practically, how does this spiritual stairstepping work? Senior-high girls can minister to junior-high teenagers. They can have slumber parties, rap sessions—all of the things girls like to do—and share practical suggestions with those befuddled seventh-, eighth-, and ninth-graders on how they themselves managed to survive that traumatic portion of their lives.

College-career age girls can minister to high schoolers, tutoring them in academics and giving spiritual guidance about dating, career selection, choosing the right school, and living under the umbrella of parental, school, and employer authority. Young marrieds can help prepare their single counterparts for both the pitfalls and pleasures of married life. Young mothers can help young married women without children learn the critical basics about birth control, pregnancy, and the blessings and endurances of motherhood. Older mothers can give younger ones the benefit of their vast experiences as wives and mothers.

Working women can delineate the pros and cons of being employed outside of the home to ones who think they may want to enter the job market. Widows can teach invaluable lessons to all of their female counterparts about survival and restructuring a life. Older women can help middle-aged ones through the traumas of

GROWING, SHARING, SERVING

menopause and what to do when you're left alone with your husband after twenty-five years of kids and chaos. Women who have walked miles with the Master can show others how to grow spiritually. "This is what God has taught me" isn't wasted but fully utilized in the lives of all of the women in the church.

Read Titus 2:3-5 and list all the things the passage says women should be doing as part of their ministries to other women.

_____

_____

CONTENT

What is the content of such a ministry? That is also outlined in Titus 2:3-5. Older women are to teach the younger ones both by example and word. They are to teach them from God's Word how to behave modestly, control their speech and actions, and become godly women.

This is to be a ministry of encouragement "that (the older women) may *encourage* the younger ones." Life can be very discouraging. Suicides in the eighteen-to-twenty-five-year age group climb higher yearly. Many well-intentioned young women in our churches are immodest both in action and speech and don't know how to be good wives or mothers. And many older ladies in the same churches condemn those whom they should be discipling and directing. They say they can't understand

The Concept of Women's Ministries

what's happening to young people today. The young women have no one to look to for guidance or help and become discouraged.

Many of our most dynamic, young, Christian women are defeated and discouraged because they haven't been properly taught. Whose fault is that? Is it their mothers', who didn't raise them properly? Does the blame lie with schools that didn't teach them correctly? Or with the pastor, whose sermons don't seem to reach them? Perhaps. But the fault also lies at the feet of older Christian women who have not accepted their God-given role within their local churches to teach what is good and encourage these young women "to love their husbands, to love their children, to be sensible, pure, workers at home, kind, being subject to their own husbands, that the word of God may not be dishonored."

We are, according to this command, responsible for others' failure. We dare not sit back and complain about and condemn them when it is we who are at fault.

The content of a women's ministry is as follows: good teaching, first by example and then by using the Bible to teach these young women godly principles to live by. We are to *encourage* them, using God's Word as a basis, to be sensible and pure; to show them how to combat the enticement of sin and learn to be controlled by the Spirit rather than by the flesh or the whims of society. We are to *encourage* them in their God-given roles as wives, mothers, and homemakers; to love and have a positive, eternal effect in the lives of the people closest to them.

If we don't, the Bible says that the Word of God will be dishonored! That means that someone, somewhere, can point to a young woman from your church who, dressed in a braless tank top and tight jeans, is dragging her screaming toddler down the aisle of the supermarket yelling at him to shut up. The observer could say, "If

GROWING, SHARING, SERVING

that's what being a Christian is, who wants it?" If we have not tried to encourage and teach these younger women whom God, in His sovereign wisdom, has set in our midst, we are to blame for their misconduct.

Use this checklist of items from Titus 2:3-5 to see what ministries you might want to be a part of in your local church.
1. Women teaching women about purity and the separated life. ____
2. Women purposely exposing themselves to new Christians or to women who are less knowledgeable about Christian conduct, to set an example of reverent behavior. ____
3. Classes for women of all ages, encompassing both Bible teaching and the practical areas of a woman's life, in which they share with and encourage one another. ____
4. The more mature women teaching young mothers how to be good homemakers and wives. ____
5. Ministries that overlap age barriers and develop a sense of unity among all of the women in the church. ____

PRACTICING THE CONCEPT

If every church in this country practiced the concept and content of Titus 2:3-5, women within the Christian community would be unified in purpose, effective and blessed in their service, and would bear remaining fruit as the result of their commitment to the challenge God has given them. There would be no limit to what we

The Concept of Women's Ministries

could accomplish for His honor and glory.

What must we do to initially implement this ministry? The first, important step is to establish a discipleship ministry so that the older women can minister to the younger ones. Undoubtedly these kinds of relationships already exist in your church. And they probably started when a more mature woman saw a need in a younger one and took her under her wing.

Discipleship in a women's ministry is a unique combination of friendship, motherhood, and education. It is assessing the needs in the life of one woman, then matching her with another who has the wisdom, practical experience, and spiritual understanding to direct, guide, and love her disciple toward maturity.

Look up the word *disciple* in a dictionary and write out the definition.

_____

_____

In Greek, the language in which the New Testament was written, the word for *disciple* is *mathetes*. It means a learner or one who follows, one who is trained. It is different from the word *didaskalos*, which means "teacher." Discipleship is more than teaching.

Frequently the concept of discipleship is misunderstood. Sometimes women have told me they could not disciple anyone because they were not teachers. While a legitimate part of discipleship may be based in Bible study, that is not the essence of it. In 1 Thessalonians 1:6-8 Paul defines a disciple as someone who becomes an imitator of her discipler and of the Lord and, in turn, becomes a godly example to other believers.

GROWING, SHARING, SERVING

How does this work in a women's ministry? If a younger woman doesn't know how to be a good mother, she is assigned to an older one who is successfully raising a family. Her discipler does not teach lessons about being a mother, but she sets an example by spending time with her younger counterpart and showing her the principles of discipline and common sense that make motherhood a joy.

Nancy didn't know how to prepare a grocery list and shop the ads. So we made out our shopping lists, and I took her to the store with me a few times; and she, by following my example, learned how to be a frugal shopper.

Linda couldn't organize her time effectively. She got help from Lois, who suggested that Linda keep a diary for one week, recording how she spent every fifteen-minute segment of her day. Linda saw how she was wasting time, and Lois noted that Linda had a tendency to start several things at once but never complete any of them. Lois shared how she organizes her time, and now Linda isn't only a better "worker at home" with a happier husband, but she has time to pursue some of her personal interests.

Jo and Amy have been of indescribable help to young women whose husbands are into drugs or alcohol, because their husbands are dry alcoholics. They've been there and can offer wise, empathetic insights that make it possible for other Christian women to survive the horrors of such experiences.

It is easy to set up this initial discipling ministry. All a church needs to do is assess the needs and giftedness of its women, then match them in a discipleship assignment. The following form is one several churches have used.

When assignments are made, it is the responsibility of

The Concept of Women's Ministries

TO BE DISCIPLED

IF YOU ARE INTERESTED IN BEING DISCIPLED BY ANOTHER WOMAN, PLEASE FILL OUT THE FOLLOWING FORM.

Name _____

Address _____

_____

Phone _____ Married _____ Single _____

Engaged _____ Student _____

Availability: evenings _____

days AM _____ PM _____

On the back, please list particular areas where you feel you need discipling. What do you wish to gain from this relationship?

TO DISCIPLE

IF YOU ARE INTERESTED IN BEFRIENDING AND/OR DISCIPLING ANOTHER WOMAN, PLEASE FILL OUT THE FOLLOWING.

Name _____

Address _____

Phone _____ Age _____ Working Status _____

Marital Status _____

Availability: evenings _____ days AM _____ PM _____

Please list particular practical and/or spiritual areas in which you're especially qualified and feel you could be of service to another woman.

GROWING, SHARING, SERVING

the older woman to contact her disciple and further the relationship. She offers herself as a friend, a surrogate mother, and an educator who through patience and example helps and encourages a sister in Christ. She, in turn, gets a friend, a surrogate daughter or sister and someone to learn from, too. Isn't it worth a try?

WORKSHOP

Does your church have any sort of women's ministry? It may not be called by that name, but there are probably many activities in which women are involved. In the spaces below, list as many women's functions and organizations as you can and describe the basic purpose of each class or group.

Name of Group	Purpose

List any needs you know of that are not being met.

_____
_____
_____

The Concept of Women's Ministries

1 Timothy 3:8-11 lists some common qualities for men and women who want to serve in the church. List those qualities below, using your own words.

_____

_____

_____

1 Peter 3:3-4 lists another very important quality a Christian woman should possess. Rewrite these verses in your own words, describing the important attitude.

_____

_____

Look up each passage and write what the woman in it did in her ministry.
Matthew 27:55-56 _____
Mark 12:41-44 _____
Mark 14:3-8 _____
Luke 8:1-3 _____
Luke 10:39 _____
John 4:28-29, 39 _____
Acts 1:12-14 _____
Acts 18:1-3, 18 _____
Acts 18:24-26 _____
Romans 16:3-5 _____

49

THE PRISCILLA PRINCIPLE
4

NOW THAT WE HAVE ESTABLISHED that you should become a ministering woman, how can you effectively serve in your church and community? Let's take a look at the pattern of one of the women in the early church—Priscilla.

In Acts 18:1-4 we read that she and her husband, Aquila, took in the apostle Paul and labored in practical areas with him, in this case, tentmaking. The principle we see here is that God expects all of us, male or female, to take care of the responsibilities of our homes and jobs before we try to expand into any kind of far-reaching ministry.

Priscilla was a coworker with her husband and Paul.

The Priscilla Principle

The Priscilla principle is that a ministering woman must not try to strike out on her own, but should willingly and cheerfully work with and beside her mate, if that is possible, and also with the church leaders. God will use them to guide and direct what she does.

Priscilla also helped teach the Word of God. "Now a certain Jew named Apollos, an Alexandrian by birth, an eloquent man, came to Ephesus; and he was mighty in the Scriptures. This man had been instructed in the way of the Lord; and being fervent in spirit, he was speaking and teaching accurately the things concerning Jesus, being acquainted only with the baptism of John; and he began speaking out boldly in the synagogue. But when Priscilla and Aquila heard him, they took him aside and explained to him the way of God more accurately" (Acts 18:24-26).

Priscilla was able to help a very knowledgeable man. She did not serve tea and crumpets while Aquila discipled Apollos. She was equally as capable and available as her husband and was a coworker in Christ with him. Priscilla's pattern illustrates that women can certainly have effective teaching ministries in the church.

Priscilla must have had a dramatic effect on many lives, including that of the apostle Paul. In Romans 16:3-5 he calls her a fellow-worker in Christ Jesus and notes that she was a lady of courage who risked her life to help him. She helped establish churches, and she and Aquila had a church in their home. She was well remembered and appreciated as a woman who labored for God in adverse circumstances. God still needs women like Priscilla.

How can you be a Priscilla in your church? List five things you believe the Bible says a woman can do in her local church.

GROWING, SHARING, SERVING

1. _____
2. _____
3. _____
4. _____
5. _____

List some areas in which you have served in the past.

_____

_____

List an area in which you would like to serve in the future.

_____

SALVATION: THE INITIAL SHARING OF THE GOSPEL

A personal relationship with Christ is the most basic need anyone has. You can give advice, quote Bible verses, give money, and do all sorts of good deeds, but unless a person is introduced to Christ, he or she will continue to walk in darkness and, ultimately, go to hell. So evangelism is an extremely important ministry, and it is one in which God uses women in a special way. Psalm 68:11 declares that "the Lord gives the command; the women who proclaim the good tidings are a great host."

The Samaritan woman at the well was so affected by Jesus Christ that she "left her waterpot, and went into the city, and said to the men [whom she had been avoiding because she was a moral and social outcast], 'Come, see a man who told me all the things that I have done; this is not the Christ, is it?' . . . And from that city many of the

The Priscilla Principle

Samaritans believed in Him because of the word of the woman who testified" (John 4:28-29, 39).

How can you actively participate in an evangelism ministry? If your church has a formal outreach program, you can serve in it. You can offer to call on visitors or on the sick. You can bring unsaved people to church. Make a point of asking everyone you meet or talk to if they are a Christian, or ask them what someone has to do to become a Christian. You will be surprised at how many witnessing doors can be opened because of that question.

Also, you should not assume that everyone who comes to church is saved; many unregenerate souls come through those sanctuary doors. I learned that the hard way.

Judy had attended my morning Bible class for about two years, and she started bringing her neighbor, who was of a different faith. Judy was very excited as she told me how she and her neighbor were praying and studying the Bible together every day. She said, "It is so wonderful to have another Christian to share with!"

So Judy's neighbor also started attending my class. After she had come for several months, she called and asked if she could make a counseling appointment with me. I set one up, assuming she had a marriage problem or difficulties with her children. I was dumbfounded when her first statement was, "I know you'll probably think I'm pretty slow, but over and over in class you talk about being a Christian, and Judy calls me one, but I don't know what a Christian is."

I was both ashamed and embarrassed that I had been so negligent in my evangelism ministry. I had forgotten a principle my friend Georgia Lee taught me years before—never assume anyone is a Christian; always confirm that they are.

GROWING, SHARING, SERVING

One legitimate way you can be a Priscilla in your church is to share the good news, the gospel. Write out the definition of the word *evangelism* here.

_____

_____

Finish this sentence. I, (name) _____, can help in the initial sharing of the gospel in my church by __

_____

Write a short paragraph telling what Christ has done for you personally (such as changed a bad temper, made you more peaceful, or taught you how to be unselfish), then share it with two people you talk to in church in the next month.

COUNSELING: TEACHING PEOPLE TO USE SCRIPTURE IN A PRACTICAL WAY

The Bible is not a book you read; it is a book you do. Its sixty-six books were written over a period of sixteen hundred years in three languages by forty authors, many of whom did not know one another; yet it maintains a unified theme and purpose and a continuity of teaching. It is unique because it is holy, inerrant, and was authored by God. Beyond any of this is the mind-boggling fact that "the word of God is living and active" (Heb. 4:12). It breathes and moves, motivates and guides; therefore, it is the best tool to use for counseling.

To be a Christian counselor, we do not have to have a degree in psychology or a lot of worldly knowledge. On the contrary we are warned to "see to it that no one takes you captive through philosophy and empty deception, according to the tradition of men, according to the

The Priscilla Principle

elementary principles of the world, rather than according to Christ" (Col. 2:8). So Christian counseling is not telling people how to solve their problems or throwing the latest theory at someone. Very simply, it is teaching others how to solve problems and get answers through the use of God's Word. Any Christian who knows the Bible and has applied it in his or her life can counsel another person.

I am not saying there is not a place for trained counselors in the Body of Christ, but I do believe any Christian who knows and is obedient to the Word can offer help to another. Too often we think of counseling as a formal, rigid interview. All it actually is, is sharing experiences and discussing how God's stated wisdom can be applied in any situation.

For example, if a friend confides to you that she and her husband are having trouble with a disobedient child, you can share verses from Proverbs, Colossians, and Ephesians and tell what you have done in similar situations. You can help her think through how she and her husband can apply the scriptural principles you discussed.

You can be sure you are doing what is beneficial for someone when you teach them to use Scripture to solve problems. 2 Timothy 3:16-17 tells what the living Word can do in a person's life. First it says, "All Scripture is inspired by God." That means if we use the Bible as a resource, rather than imposing our own opinions, God will be supplying the answers, and they will be infallible.

Next we are told that Scripture is profitable for teaching, which is initial instruction. We can use it to teach someone something he or she never knew before. Second, it is profitable for reproof, weeding out the true from the untrue, testing ideas and beliefs, making sure they coincide with Scripture.

GROWING, SHARING, SERVING

Third, it is profitable for correction, for changing from wrong to right. Fourth, it is worthwhile for training in righteousness. We can use it to give further knowledge for future use in godly living; to learn things we may not need right at the moment but that we will face in time. The end result of such counsel is "that the [woman] of God may be adequate, equipped for every good work" (2 Tim. 3:17).

I am not formally trained as a counselor, but I do a lot of counseling. From one nonprofessional to another, here is my basic approach. First, find out if the person is a Christian. If not, salvation is the basic issue. Next, ask that person to look up with you what the Bible says about their problem. To do this you will need to know some verses on topics such as worry, fear, finances, marriage, children, honesty, and all the other areas where our humanity defeats us. End by discussing what alternatives are open to them. Have them actually list on paper the options that are available.

Priscilla counseled Apollos as part of her ministry. List one area in your life in which you have some practical experience and biblical knowledge that could be helpful to share with someone.

TEACHING: SHARING GOD'S WORD WITH OTHERS

Teaching is passing on knowledge, but in contrast to counseling, it is a positive ministry. Teaching is instruction before a problem arises rather than offering solu-

The Priscilla Principle

tions after a crisis exists. Teaching can be on a one-on-one basis, in a small group, or in a large body. A woman can teach children, women, and sometimes, men. One who teaches in a formal position should have the spiritual gift of teaching. Whatever anyone teaches should undergird the church's pulpit ministry.

Above all, we must be students of the Word if we are going to teach it. We should be dedicated to sharing truths from the Bible, not our own pet theories. What we teach should closely match the statement of faith of our church, even if we teach in our home. We all need training in teaching methods, and the best way to get that training, even if we want to teach adults, is to teach children for at least a year.

Some people want to teach because it is a more "showy" ministry. To keep us from seeking it for the wrong reasons, God offers this warning: "Let not many of you become teachers, my brethren, knowing that as such we shall incur a stricter judgment" (James 3:1). If you think God wants you in a teaching ministry, try your wings by teaching a children's Sunday school class. If you are truly called to teach, it won't matter to you what age audience God gives you.

If you think you might want to teach, this list may help you decide. Fill in the answer that best fits you: yes, sometimes, seldom, no.

1. I enjoy studying. _____
2. People respond to me when I share ideas. _____
3. I have a deep desire to pass on to others what I have learned about the Lord. _____
4. Others tell me I should be teaching. _____
5. I have had fruit in sharing Bible truths with others. _____
6. I am at ease with a group. _____

GROWING, SHARING, SERVING

Now, list as many reasons as you can why you think you should be a teacher.

_____

_____

DISCIPLESHIP: DUPLICATING AND DEVELOPING

In the last chapter we discussed the importance of a discipleship ministry for women. The apostle Paul instructed the Corinthians to "be imitators of me, just as I am also of Christ" (1 Cor. 11:1). Simply stated, discipleship is our imitating the Lord Jesus Christ and then motivating others to imitate us: duplicating and developing ourselves in others. The first thing Christ did when He started His earthly ministry was to choose and train twelve men to do what He was doing. And His last spoken charge to us was to go and make disciples.

Discipling is being used by the Holy Spirit as a godly model to help mold someone else. Discipling is what we do with people who come to Christ and want to grow. In my case, I have several women who can speak and teach in my place. I trained them by having them help me prepare the lessons I teach, taking them with me when I go to speak, having them critique my presentations, and by turning responsibilities over to them. I also share problems and difficulties and ask them to pray for and with me and to help me look for solutions.

As a result, I have a team of women who do what I do, but who do it better and more effectively than I. Irene ministers in the area of discipleship, Shirley in practical arts, Jo in counseling, Nancy in women's ministries in a seminary and on a church staff, Dolores in Bible study techniques, and Emarie in ministries to women who are married to unbelievers. Each one's ministry duplicates a facet of mine, yet is more refined and inclusive than anything I do in those areas. Each is an expert in her field.

If there is someone you think you would like to disciple, you do not walk up to them and say, "By the way, I want you to start patterning your life and ministry after me." You challenge them with your life-style. You watch for women who have gifts and desires similar to yours—kindred spirits—and then build friendships and encourage them to develop their potential. Who would you like to minister to in this way?

AVAILABILITY: THE THING THAT MATTERS MOST

It has been said that the only ability God needs from us is our availability. We do not have to run all over trying to find things to do. All we have to do is meet existing needs, whatever they may be; the Lord will set up our ministries.

Quite a few years ago, after I had become aware of my Spirit-planted desire to teach women, I was offered a position on the board of the women's fellowship group in my church: chairman in charge of reading missionary letters every month. My first reaction was "Yuk." I had seen the audience reaction when the letters were read: one immense yawn.

But rather than say no, I said I would pray about it. So I prayed, and as I did I started thinking about how important it was for a missionary organization to identify with

GROWING, SHARING, SERVING

and have personal concern for the missionaries who wrote those letters. We needed to respond as individuals to their needs.

I decided I would take the job, if the board would let me feature one missionary family each month, telling something about the country where they were serving and their needs at the moment. I also asked to do a devotion to go with the letter reading. That was the start of my public speaking career. And I still use material from the devotional messages I prepared when I was chairman in charge of reading missionary letters.

I was available, so God used what I did to develop me toward what He had planned for me. We need to know our role, our gifts, and be there; He will create the opportunities.

WORKSHOP

What motivations or commands do each of these verses give you personally?

Evangelism: 2 Peter 3:9 _____

_____

Counseling: Galatians 6:2 _____

_____

Teaching: 2 Timothy 2:2 _____

_____

Discipleship: Matthew 28:19-20 _____

_____

Availability: Isaiah 6:8 _____

_____

THE GIFTS GOD HAS GIVEN US
5

Do you remember the first time you drove a car? My first attempt was down a country road in Kansas, and it was a very traumatic event. I ground the gears and stalled the engine. I remember my dad said to me, "If you can just get going, the rest is easy." He was right. Last year I drove over ten thousand miles and thought nothing of it. I do it almost automatically.

The same principle can apply in anything we do: if we can just get going, the rest is easy. So, in the next few chapters we're going to do some possibility exploration and develop a philosophy that leads to performance. We're going to look at ways to get our ministries going and how to gain momentum.

GROWING, SHARING, SERVING
POSSIBILITY EXPLORATION

What is possibility exploration? It is looking forward, not behind, and discovering all the opportunities that are open. It is replacing such words as *depression, indecision, frustration, apathy,* and *boredom* with words like *challenge, excitement, action,* and *fulfillment*. Possibility exploration is seeing every situation as a God-given circumstance for growth. It is moving from where we are to where God wants us to be and, on the way, enlarging our capacity both to feel and to do. It is building a philosophy for action into our lives.

As cliched as it sounds, the essence of possibility exploration is learning to look for opportunities and then acting on them. The secret of success is to become a Romans 8:28 thinker: to believe and act in faith on the fact that "God causes all things to work together for good to those who love God, to those who are called according to His purpose." We train ourselves to remember that behind every problem is a blessing, every so-called defeat is a progression, and every catastrophe holds an encouragement.

That is not to say there are no negatives, but there are positives in the negatives if we will only look for them. We can learn to live as if a great adventure, leading to accomplishment, is lurking in the midst of each moment that passes.

I have found that the worst problems conceal the greatest joys. When I had to leave a secular teaching position because I had been openly sharing my faith in Christ, God opened the way for my Christian teaching ministry. When my husband George had a heart attack and open-heart surgery, I learned more about the power of prayer and surrender to God's will than I could have in

The Gifts God Has Given Us

pleasant circumstances. And God used that near tragedy to make me reassess my priorities and gain a new perspective about what is important and what isn't. We'll talk more about how to handle problems in the next chapter.

ACTIVATED ABILITIES

Possibility exploration is not based entirely on circumstances. It also involves using our minds and abilities. Most people are created with a multitude of talents, but these differ in each individual. My husband is extremely talented in math and in analytical and mechanical areas. I am artistic with words. One of my friends has an eye for texture and color and has a flair for decorating. Another is a gourmet cook.

The point is that we all have certain natural talents and abilities to be developed. It is important to discover what our own talents are, so we can put them to proper use.

List eight of your natural talents. Don't be modest. (Incidentally, these do not need to be showy or bring attention to you. Just things you know and appreciate about yourself.)

1. _____ 5. _____
2. _____ 6. _____
3. _____ 7. _____
4. _____ 8. _____

When a person becomes a Christian, God also bestows spiritual gifts. There are several theological schools of thought about spiritual gifts. One is that each Christian gets only one gift. Another is that a multiplicity of gifts is

GROWING, SHARING, SERVING

given to each believer. Still another is that each person gets one major gift and others, less prominent, to help minister in that more gifted area. The important thing to know about gifts is that everyone has at least one, given by Christ, to be used for His glory. "Christ has given each of us special abilities—whatever he wants us to have—out of his rich storehouse of gifts" (Eph. 4:7, TLB).

What does each of these passages teach about the purpose of your gifts?

Romans 12:4-6 _____

1 Corinthians 12:4-7 _____

Ephesians 4:12 _____

What are the gifts? Some of the ones listed in the Bible that you might identify in your life, include: *faith*, which is desiring and seeking what is in accordance with God's will. This gift is frequently seen in someone who has an active, effective prayer life. *Prophecy* is the gift of stating revealed truth in power, guided by the Holy Spirit. The gift of *ministry* is serving in an "above and beyond" way to the needs of all believers. *Exhortation* is counseling: using the Word of God to help and give practical aid to others. Some other gifts are *teaching*, which is instructing people in the Word; *giving*, which is unselfish sharing of financial and other resources for God's glory, as the Spirit directs; *ruling*, which is administrating the tasks God assigns, delegating authority and helping organize so things run smoothly and well.

The gift of *mercy*, is inspired acts that manifest the love of Christ. Some people with this gift literally suffer through problems with others, hurting and crying with

The Gifts God Has Given Us

them. It is the ability to be empathetic in the keenest sense.

Finally, there are the gifts of *wisdom*, which is clearly stating and applying spiritual truth, a kind of insightfulness into how to live in accord with Scripture; *knowledge*, which is the ability to know the true facts; *discernment*, which is being able to decide what is of God and what is of Satan; and *helps*, which is aiding and physically lending support in the everyday areas of life. People with the gift of helps are the ones who clean the church nursery, collect clothes for the missionaries, paint the walls, baby-sit your children while you teach your Bible class, and who bring the pot of chicken soup when you have the flu.

All gifts are equally necessary and important. Paul makes it very clear that they are given by the Spirit, to be ministered to the Lord, brought into effectiveness by God and are "for the common good" (1 Cor. 12:7) of the church. If you have never identified what your gifts are, look at your performance, and the general areas in which you serve fruitfully and enjoyably, for clues.

Look over the preceding list of spiritual gifts, and write down one you think you might have. Tell why you think you are gifted in this area and how you have used your gift in the past.

_____
_____
_____
_____
_____

GROWING, SHARING, SERVING

SPIRIT-PLANTED DESIRES

Knowing that we have both natural and spiritual gifts should make it easier for us to explore various possibilities. The question for each of us is, what will I do with those talents and gifts; how can I start moving out in the ministry God has prepared for me? How do I get going?

Put this book aside for a moment, close your eyes, and think. What is something you have always wanted to do to serve the Lord? No matter how crazy or different it might be, think about it. It may be something you have pushed to the back of your mind for many years or a dream you have never shared with anyone because you thought it was too farfetched to have any merit. Ask the Holy Spirit to help you think creatively.

I call these kinds of ideas, ones you have thought about and dismissed as impossible, Spirit-planted desires. Psalm 37:4 says, "Delight yourself in the Lord; and He will give you the desires of your heart." God plants those dreams, wants, wishes, visions, and "if only I could's" in us if we are delighting in Him. Why is it we think that if something appeals to us, it must be wrong? How many times have we quenched our Spirit-planted desires?

I love to see the looks on the faces of the women in my workshop seminars as they start thinking about what they've really wanted to do, about the dreams they've buried in a box labeled "impossible." It is as if a light has gone on in their souls.

The first time I was aware of a Spirit-planted desire, I thought I was sinning. My dear friend Georgia Lee, who is a Christian actress and speaker, was standing in the podium at a large conference center, speaking to about eight hundred women. As I watched her I remember

The Gifts God Has Given Us

thinking, "Someday I want to do what she is doing. I want to talk to huge groups of women about the Lord."

When I realized what I was thinking, I guiltily looked around to see if anyone had sensed my "envy." I was ashamed and asked God to forgive me for coveting my friend's position. But that desire did not go away; rather, it grew in intensity. And several years later, when I was standing at that same podium, teaching about eight hundred women, I recounted the story with tears in my eyes. I knew by then I wasn't covetous, because I in no way wanted to detract from or interfere with Georgia Lee's ministry. I knew that the Holy Spirit of God had planted that desire in my heart and then had brought it to pass.

He will do the same for you. Bill Bright had a desire to see the entire world evangelized, and he began Campus Crusade for Christ International. Henrietta Mears had a desire to develop a Bible-teaching Christian retreat center for men, women, and children, and she founded Forest Home Christian Conference Center. David C. Cook I had a desire to see quality Sunday school curriculum put into churches, and he organized a publishing company. Luis Palau had a desire to see South and Central America taught the truth of the Word of God, and his preaching ministry has been used by the Lord to bring hundreds of thousands of people to a knowledge of Christ. These men and women were no different than you and I. They committed their lives to acting on the Spirit-planted desires God had given them, believing He is the God of the impossible.

Our ministries begin when we act on our Spirit-planted desires. Fill in the blanks below.
1. One of my Spirit-planted desires is _____

GROWING, SHARING, SERVING

2. I have had this desire for (length of time) _____
3. Three things I can do to get going are _____
   _____

(Remember, I did not start out by teaching over eight hundred women from that podium where my friend stood. I started by teaching a Sunday school class of second-grade boys and leading a small, struggling home Bible study.)

4. Now write a prayer, asking God to lead you step by step in fulfilling His desire for you and in using the giftedness He has given to you.

_____
_____
_____

5. Write the name of one other person with whom you will share your Spirit-planted desire and whom you will ask to pray for you.

_____

6. Memorize Psalm 37:4, Amplified Bible: "Delight yourself also in the Lord, and He will give you the desires and secret petitions of your heart."

WORKSHOP

Look up each passage and write one thing it says about spiritual giftedness.

1 Corinthians 7:7 _____
_____

The Gifts God Has Given Us

1 Peter 4:10-11 _____
_____

1 Corinthians 12:14-25 _____
_____

Ephesians 4:16 _____
_____

1 Corinthians 12:11 _____
_____

1 Timothy 4:14 _____
_____

THE POSITIVES IN NEGATIVES
6

EVERY PERSON I KNOW, or have studied about in history classes, or have heard about in today's news, who has made something of herself or himself has believed in some way that *problems are not obstacles but opportunities*.

Periodically, in the *Los Angeles Times*, one of the local department stores runs an advertisement for "Nearly Me," a unique breast prosthesis. Beside it is a picture of a radiant, smiling woman. The ad says, "Nearly Me was developed by Ruth Handler, also inventor of the Barbie Doll, who herself has had a mastectomy." I have never met Ruth Handler, but that sentence tells me she is a courageous lady who saw a devastating problem as an opportunity to use her misfortune and talents to help others.

The Positives in Negatives

In our humanity we tend to think of problems as deterrents that make it impossible to complete our plans. We see them as limitations, as obstacles in the path of our progress. But that is not true. Charles Swindoll, a well-known pastor, has said, "We are all faced with great opportunities cleverly disguised as insolvable problems." In other words, the *real* problem isn't the problem but our attitude about it.

To practice possibility exploration, we must train ourselves to look for the opportunity in the problem rather than to look at the problem itself. Josh Billings said, "Opportunity is where it is found and seldom where it is sought." He had learned that while it is unwise to go looking for opportunities, he could expect to find them right where he was at any given moment.

Problems are God's way of keeping us moving. Instead of learning or exploring, a satisfied person sits back, takes it easy, and does not look for new directions to take *until* God throws a difficulty in the path. After a heartbreaking series of failures in his experiments, Thomas Edison told a coworker, "We haven't failed. We now know one thousand things that won't work, so we are that much closer to finding out what will." We owe the phonograph, electric light, and moving pictures to Edison's inventiveness, which was never quenched by what appeared to be insolvable problems.

When you are caught in a so-called problem, you can turn it into an opportunity if you *act* on it rather than *reacting* to it. For example, if someone is consistently and unkindly critical of you, you can react by blowing up, being hurt, and returning criticisms. Or, you can act on the criticisms by evaluating their validity and figuring out what you can do to stop the attacks.

I recall a time in my life when God was ready for me to resign a certain position and move on to other things.

GROWING, SHARING, SERVING

Down deep I knew this was His desire, but I had many good surface reasons why I should not do it. I was in a prestigious position, was having a very fruitful ministry, making good money, receiving recognition, and doing what I had waited many years to be able to do. I was also ignoring God's will. So He lovingly put problem after problem in my path—not to stop me from ministering—but to help me minister more fully, and to put me where He wanted me to be.

I was more resistant than I normally would have been because He was revealing His will to me through two people whom I knew were not supportive of me as a person nor of the job I was doing. The more I resisted and the more I got bogged down in the difficulty, the more critical they became. And I was doing exactly what I have just advised you not to do; I reacted to the situation rather than acting upon it.

Then one night at a meeting, one of the people who had been opposing me clearly stated that he did not think God wanted me in the position I held. I do not know what happened, but somehow I was finally able to separate the message from the messenger, and I realized that God was showing me His will through someone I felt was an enemy. I had rejected what I was being told because of the source. When I accepted it, I saw the many opportunities the Lord had in store for me. And I learned two important lessons: no one but Jo Berry can stop me from doing what God has planned for me, and God's truth must be accepted regardless of how it comes packaged!

In Acts 16, Paul and Silas had what most of us would consider a problem. They had been jailed on false charges. But then there was a great earthquake, and everyone's chains were unfastened. When the jailer realized what had happened, he was going to kill himself

The Positives in Negatives

because he was so sure all of the prisoners had escaped. But Paul stopped him, saying, "Do yourself no harm, for we are all here" (Acts 16:28). Paul and Silas stayed and witnessed to the jailer, and he accepted Christ, along with his entire household.

Paul and Silas viewed imprisonment as an opportunity, not an obstacle. If they had run for the door the moment the chains were broken, certain that God had released them, they could not have been used to bring the jailer to salvation. They did not run from their problem but seized the chance to share the gospel instead.

Problems are not obstacles but opportunities! God uses them to show us what He wants us to do and to put us where He wants us to be. In my case He wanted me to move on to something else, and I was stubbornly staying. He wanted Paul and Silas to stay when they could have gone. But in both instances, He used an apparent problem to direct and guide as well as produce positive results.

To help start internalizing this concept, answer these questions:
1. What is one of the biggest problems you are presently facing?

_____

_____

2. What did you do or are you doing to cause or contribute to the problem?

_____

_____

3. What is one positive action you can take to help solve it?

_____

4. Will worry, anger, or guilt help? _____

GROWING, SHARING, SERVING

5. What opportunities are in this problem?
_____
_____

6. How might God be using this to redirect you in your life or ministry?
_____

THE FRIENDLY FOE

Our attitude about time is another important part of possibility exploration. We are so impatient that we frequently view time as an enemy, a factor that works against us. But the Bible teaches that impatience is our enemy and time is an ally, an earthly gift given to us by God to be used in the here and now.

Ecclesiastes 3:1 says, "There is an appointed time for everything. And there is a time for every event under heaven." Sometimes we miss appointed possibilities to minister because we jump ahead of (or lag behind) God's perfect scheduling in our lives. God knows exactly when it is best for us to do something, and if we are going too fast, He will slow us down, and if we are poking along, He will set the circumstances so we must speed up our timetable.

As we start to act upon our Spirit-planted desires, we need to remember that there is an appointed time for everything. If something does not work out the way we want, when we want it to, God is not necessarily telling us to drop the idea; He may be urging us to look at His timetable.

Recently I heard Anne Ortlund speak about the importance of timing. She shared three things to help us stay in line with God's perfect appointment calendar. She said we should learn to eliminate our obvious failures, because God is probably saying He does not want us to waste our time on things we have tried and tried that have not come to fruition. She said we should also eliminate our present successes, because doing the same things over and over will not encourage us to grow and follow after the new things God has for us to do. Finally, she advised that we postpone future successes until God is ready for them to happen. Our awareness of Spirit-planted desires may precede their implementation by months or even years.

Time is an ally in several ways. Time prepares. All of us need to learn, especially when we are motivated to do something, that it takes time to lay solid, permanent foundations. This has been a hard fact for me to accept. I see something that needs to be done, and I want to do it yesterday. I am a perfect example of fools rushing in where angels fear to tread. But God is teaching me the immense value of slow, thorough, methodical preparation.

In one church in which I have been helping set up a women's ministry, the lady in charge told me of her discouragement because things were moving so slowly. "Maybe it just isn't going to work here," she confided. I was surprised, because in my frame of reference, I felt things were developing quite rapidly. I reminded her that I had warned her that it would take about five years to build a full-blown women's ministry. I also shared that she is "selling" a new concept to her church and that winning support does not happen quickly. Education is a slow process, demanding much repetition. Doing anything well takes time.

Time is also an ally because it heals. Some things are

GROWING, SHARING, SERVING

erased or eased only by time. When you realize that time will take care of the past, you can focus on the present and the future. Time also befriends us by being useful. We need it for order and meaning in life. It brackets change. And, time is an ally because it encourages. Nothing on earth is forever. There is always another day. So if you fail or miss an opportunity, you can take heart, because there is always tomorrow.

Timing is important. Dreams do not always die; sometimes we kill them by giving up too soon. I know of two women who want a women's ministry in their church so badly that they are praying together about it for several hours each week. They would like to dive in and start Bible studies, discipleship programs, and practical arts courses; but instead they are wisely serving on the board of an existing women's fellowship group, planting seeds and ideas about what the women could be doing. Their goal for the next year is to start a small home Bible study to lay the groundwork. One of them told me, "If God wants this to happen sooner, it will." These ladies are using time as an ally.

Describe God's perfect timing as it is described in Ecclesiastes 3:1-8.

_____
_____
_____

Now, write out what each of these verses says about time:
Psalm 31:15a _____
Psalm 69:13 _____
Ephesians 5:15-16 _____
Acts 1:7 _____

The Positives in Negatives

ALTERNATIVE THINKING

The old adage says, "There is more than one way to skin a cat." In exploring possibilities we would do well to remember that. When one path is blocked or a door is slammed shut, it does not mean we are finished. It does mean we must find another way to "skin the cat." This is alternative thinking.

Many people predetermine in their minds what they are going to do, and if they can't, for whatever reasons, they decide God does not want them to do it. They operate on the fallacious premise of the closed-door theory, which assumes that if God wants me to do something, He will open a door for me to walk through, and if He closes a door, then I am not supposed to do it.

There are problems with this theory. First, many times there are several doors open at once. Usually you have chances to do more than one thing at any given time. So what do you do if there are four, five, or ten doors open? You cannot walk through all of them. Second, if you have chosen a course of action, and things do not work out, does it mean God has closed the door or that you merely tried the wrong entry at the wrong time? If you act on the closed-door theory, you will never explore all of the possibilities that are open to you.

With God there is always a way to do what He wants you to do. There is always a crack in some doorway leading to the perfect alternative route. If you operate on the closed-door theory, you could be walking by fact, not by faith. In that case, instead of wondering if the door closed so you could seek a different avenue of approach, you have stopped your quest and stoically acted on the fact that you tried a course of action and it did not work. Besides, God is not the only one who closes doors; Satan

77

has been known to slam a few, too.

There is only one thing God wants you doing at any given time, and He gave you an intellect, a will, and the indwelling of the Holy Spirit so you can determine what it is and when and how to do it. Waiting on the Lord does not mean sitting back and doing nothing. It means trusting God's perfect leading and timing as you walk the path of righteousness. "Come now, and let us reason together, says the Lord" (Isa. 1:18). We need to reason, to think of alternatives.

The following method is one I use to practice alternative thinking. Although you will be thinking of alternatives about your Spirit-planted desires and an approach to your ministry, you can also use this approach in many life situations. In any circumstance, whether shopping for a suit, a car, or deciding on a major career shift, there is always an alternative. You are never trapped. You are free in Christ.

Before you start, refer back to your list of Spirit-planted desires on page 67 and pick one you would most like to implement. Write it out.

---

1. List as many possibilities as you can, no matter how absurd they may seem or whether you believe they are possible or not, about how you can start to respond and act on the Spirit-planted desire you choose.

_____
_____
_____
_____
_____

2. Narrow the list to the realm of the possible. Eliminate

The Positives in Negatives

total impossibilities. Be realistic and hopeful.

_____

_____

_____

3. Combine alternatives if necessary.

_____

_____

Remember, there may be several acceptable solutions to the same situation. You are after God's perfect way for *you*. Whenever you do this, save your list, because if the alternative you choose does not turn out as it should, you will want to try another.

How do we learn to see the positives in negatives? By learning to recognize opportunities disguised as problems, seeing that time is a gift from God, and trusting that the alternatives He gives provide His perfect course of action for us.

What should you be praying for?

_____

_____

_____

WORKSHOP

In Romans 15:4, the apostle Paul observes that "Whatever was written in earlier times was written for our instruction, that through perseverance and the encouragement of the Scriptures we might have hope." Read each of the following references carefully; then list the negative problem the person was facing and the positive opportunity God created for him or her.

Ruth (Ruth 1—4)	Negative Problem	Positive Opportunity
Hannah (1 Sam. 1)	Negative Problem	Positive Opportunity
David (1 Sam. 17)	Negative Problem	Positive Opportunity
Esther (Esther 1—7)	Negative Problem	Positive Opportunity
Joseph (Gen. 37—39)	Negative Problem	Positive Opportunity

CREATIVE INSTIGATION
7

As I TRAVEL AND TALK with women about implementing their Spirit-planted desires, I find that many of them don't follow through on what they know God wants them to do because they simply don't know how to start. They have innovative, useful ideas, but they don't know what that crucial first step should be or what the mechanics of the initiation process are.

Ginny said, "I know many young mothers in our church desperately need instruction on how to discipline their children, but how can I say that without offending them? And how can I offer to teach a class to help them without looking like a pious know-it-all?" She tried talking to some of her peers, but she was right; they felt she was being critical and wanted no part of such a class.

Ruth saw that the age-old system for collecting and storing clothes for the missionaries was causing more problems than it was solving, and she had an idea for a simple system that would streamline collection, storage, and distribution. When she mentioned her idea ever so casually to the president of the women's missionary group, all she got was an uncordial "hrumph."

Betty wanted to set up a lending library of tapes and books, separate from the regular church library, containing materials that would give young, single girls a resource to help them solve their immediate problems. She offered to review the books and tapes and was willing to counsel the women who checked out the materials. She was told by the powers that be that this would be a confusing duplication of services and wasn't necessary.

Can such problems be averted? Can these kinds of discouragements be turned into encouragements? I believe they can, if we learn to practice creative instigation.

CREATIVE INSTIGATION

What is creative instigation? It is fitting the new into the old. It's overcoming the attitude of "But we've always done it this way." It's doing innovative things in a nonthreatening way. The principle behind creative instigation is found in 1 Corinthians 10:32-33, which says, "Give no offense either to Jews or to Greeks or to the church of God; just as I also please all men in all things, not seeking my own profit, but the profit of many, that they may be saved." Creative instigation keeps roadblocks such as Ginny, Ruth, and Betty encountered

Creative Instigation

to a minimum and gives you a course of action to follow when you come up with an idea that can revitalize or revolutionize the status quo.

HOW TO CREATIVELY INSTIGATE

There are six basic, uncomplicated steps to creative instigation.

- *Learn what exists and why it exists before you try to change it.* What you want to do may be valid and necessary, but it may not warrant a change in the existing structure. You need to know if what you are suggesting is a new concept or if it has been or is already being used in part or total. Some programs and procedures endure because they are good and useful. You need to know what is happening before you try to change it.
- *Work within the existing structure.* Wherever you are is a springboard, not a millstone. Too often we resist the system rather than using it to our advantage. Follow rules and regulations that are set up. They may seem foolish and unnecessary to you, but remember, you aren't trying to change the system but are trying to be effective and useful in it.
- *Work through existing channels.* Don't jump the chain of command or undermine others. Be willing to start at the bottom and win approval, take advice, and, at times, modify your approach. Find out who is in authority over whom and whom to approach with your ideas.

We are admonished "be obedient to those who are your masters according to the flesh, with fear and trembling, in the sincerity of your heart, as to Christ; not by way of eyeservice, as men-pleasers, but as slaves of Christ, doing the will of God from the heart" (Eph.

6: 5-6). Balking at ruling boards or bucking the chain of command is not the way to reach your goals. Working *with* people rather than against or apart from them will pave the road to success and will also win favor with others. Allies are always more helpful than enemies or competitors.

• *Listen to your superiors.* Most people in authority are there because they know what they are doing. In churches, the leaders are placed there by God and have been gifted by Him to do whatever tasks He ordains for them. Respect their experience and position. There is a wisdom, an expertise, that comes with age. People who are older or more experienced than you can teach you a lot if you're willing to learn from them and are as eager to try their ideas as you want them to be to try yours.

Four of the most important words anyone can ever say are "What do you think?" Don't look at your plans and projects as sacred territory, but ask the opinion of others; pick their brains. Bounce ideas off of them rather than lording opinions over them. It isn't always true that too many cooks spoil the broth. Sometimes the unique touch of a number of people makes a better soup.

• *Know what you are doing.* Sadly, many good ideas die before they're tested because someone foolishly tries to set a brainchild in motion before the proper groundwork has been laid. If Ginny, whom we discussed earlier, had gone to the president of her young-marrieds' Sunday school class for counsel, and had asked an older woman to team-teach with her or act as an advisor and counselor to the group, she most likely could have started a class for training mothers how to discipline their children.

If Ruth had approached the president of the women's missionary group in the right way at the right time, she might have gotten more than a disinterested "hrumph." And if Betty had been able to give the church librarian her

Creative Instigation

reasons for wanting a separate resource library in a clear, concise, direct, honest way, she might not have been refused permission to go ahead with her plans.

When you want to implement an idea, make an appointment with whomever you should contact. Do some research before the meeting so you can state what you hope to accomplish. Be ready to tell briefly and clearly *why* you want to do what you are suggesting, the results you expect, and *how* it can be done for the benefit of all concerned.

Ruth could have invited the president of the missionary group to lunch, then asked her opinion about those ideas for a different administrative approach so she would have seen Ruth's suggestion as a solution to a problem rather than as a threat to her territory. I'm sure both Mrs. Davis and Ruth wanted to get clothes to the missionaries. They had a mutual desire to serve, but Ruth's approach thwarted her purposes.

Likewise, Betty went to the library committee before she ever talked to the church librarian personally. She didn't do her public-relations work. If she'd spent fifteen minutes alone with the librarian and shared the needs she saw, had asked for help, and stated a willingness to work through the present library system rather than apart from it, she would probably have gotten her singles' resource library. Her initial contact bypassed existing channels.

- *Communication paves the way to accomplishment.* Communication involves getting *consent,* which is selling your idea and getting approval; *commitment,* which is getting permission to try your plan; and *performance,* which is doing what you feel needs to be done. If you succeed in persuading the right people to accept your plan and to commit themselves to helping you carry it out, you are on your way.

GROWING, SHARING, SERVING
ENTHUSIASM IS ESSENTIAL

If you want multiple possibilities opened to you, and if you hope to accomplish what you set out to do, remember that enthusiasm is essential. Enthusiasm can sell almost anything, can convince almost anyone. Enthusiasm motivates. If you are enthusiastic about your ideas, your potential, the potential of others, and about what God can and is doing in your life, you will get things done. If you are enthusiastic about a women's ministry and your part in it, others will catch that spark and be motivated to get involved, too.

Paul tells us to "be fervent in spirit" (Rom. 12:11). Do you know what a fervent spirit is? If you have ever boiled a pot of water, you know it eventually splatters out onto the stove or onto your hand or arm if you get too close. That is what the word *fervent* means: spewing over. If you have a fervent spirit, you are so enthused that your excitement splatters over onto others and touches their lives in a positive way. It makes them want what you've got and causes them to want to become involved in what you're doing. Enthusiasm—a fervent spirit—is essential in a ministry!

Paul J. Meyer, founder of Success Motivation Institute, Inc., has said that "a man of second-rate ability with enthusiasm will generally outstrip the one of first-rate ability without enthusiasm. True enthusiasm is a combination of two human factors: intellect and emotion. It springs from the heart and is as difficult to hide as is great sorrow or abiding love. The power of enthusiasm lies in the natural and unrestrained expression of it."[1]

Think of something you want to do in your church ministry. Have you been truly enthusiastic about it? On the lines below list five things you can fervently share

Creative Instigation

with others about your ministry idea that will create an honest excitement in them.

For example, I try to share the concept of a women's ministry with someone from every church I go into. I know:

1. The potential of many of the women in any congregation is being wasted.
2. The idea is a biblical one we have overlooked or neglected.
3. A women's ministry is a positive motivation for both men and women.
4. I have tried it and it works!
5. We should be doing more for the Lord, and a women's ministry is one way to serve more fully. So many needs are not being met.

What are your enthusiasms about your area of ministry?

1. _____
2. _____
3. _____
4. _____
5. _____

VOLUNTEERING WINS VOTES

Volunteering is another way to explore possibilities, to establish your credentials, to build a reputation as a doer, and to help you climb the ladder from where you are to where you want to be. Have you ever been in one of those awkward situations in which the poor chairperson

GROWING, SHARING, SERVING

or superintendent said, "We still haven't found anyone to do thus and such," then pathetically and pleadingly looked around and said, "Wouldn't one of you *please* . . . ?"

Some of the greatest opportunities you will ever face will come from saying, "Oh, OK, I'll do it." The more and varied experiences you have, the greater your chances for achievement. When you volunteer to do something no one else wants or sees as significant or has time for, you lay a lot of important groundwork. What you do is prove you are a person who'll step out on faith. You also create goodwill for yourself in the group and give God an opportunity to develop you into the person He wants you to be.

When I was in junior-high school, I volunteered to teach primary Sunday school. I developed a love for teaching children and gained insights into how they learn and what their needs are. Oh, I would rather have been sitting with my friends in adult church, writing notes back and forth about boys and football games and what to wear to school on Monday, but God used that situation to create a desire in me to see His little ones properly educated and taught with good, effective curriculum that meets their life needs. He used that experience, which lasted only a few months, to give impetus to things I do even now: writing Sunday school curriculum and acting as an education consultant for a Christian publisher.

A friend of mine, who is a successful author and works in the area of counseling, told me she seems to have always been plagued by a compulsion to raise her hand and volunteer her services when no one else was available. She is convinced that her willingness to dive into so many interesting and varied situations is at the root of her success.

Creative Instigation

Volunteering to do something you hadn't thought of doing, or maybe don't particularly want to do, can lead you to what you want to do. My friend Irene is a good example. She has always had a burden for discipleship: to see women built, step by step, into God's best. But she didn't start out discipling women. She began by teaching a sixth-grade girls' Sunday school class, in which she developed techniques and examined ways to meet the deep-seated needs in her students' lives. Then she began teaching a small and sometimes discouraging women's group. She told me there was a time when she was actually jealous of me, because she wanted to teach a big Bible study and be in the foreground.

But as a result of having volunteered for a job and having persistent dedication, Irene has reached her goal to disciple. She works with groups of twelve or less "because that's where the real action takes place," and has not only changed the lives of many Christian women and girls but has developed a discipleship program and written a manual that could be used to build disciples in women's ministries throughout the total Body of Christ. It started when she, not too eagerly, volunteered to teach a sixth-grade Sunday school class.

Sometime this week, make a point of finding out what kinds of volunteer positions are open in your church. You could call the office, or talk to your pastor or Sunday school teacher. Write some of the possibilities in the space below, pray about them, and volunteer to do one thing on a short-term basis.

_____
_____
_____

GROWING, SHARING, SERVING

As part of your reaching out for Christ, try to discover some volunteer positions that are open in your community. Most schools, libraries, hospitals, and charity organizations use unpaid workers. Call some of them and list the possibilities in the space below. Pray about them, and volunteer to do one thing on a short-term basis.

_____
_____
_____

The prophet Isaiah says, "I heard the voice of the Lord saying, 'Whom shall I send, and who will go for us?' Then I said, 'Here am I. Send me!' " (Isa. 6:8). Isaiah didn't know where he was going or what God was going to do through him, but he volunteered. That's what Irene and I and many women whom you know and admire have done. And as a result God used us, just as He wants to use you, to launch His perfect plan for women everywhere. How do you know you aren't the one He has chosen to develop the concept of a women's ministry in your church? Won't you say, "Here I am, Lord! Send me!"?

WORKSHOP

Let's practice creative instigation by working through a case study. Lois is a Christian woman about your age who has been a member in her church for seven years. She has taught Sunday school and served on the women's fellowship board. She is deeply concerned about the

Creative Instigation

quality of the regular women's Bible study in her church.

The lady who teaches the study, Mrs. Davidson, is almost seventy years old. She has taught the class for years and is loved and respected. She knows the Word well, but rather than teaching topical studies that would meet needs in the lives of many of the younger women in the church, she teaches mostly devotional and inspirational materials. The Bible study is presently attended by an increasingly older group of women who have been going for years and who are rather critical of the younger and newer women who do not attend.

The church is growing, and many families have joined in the last three years. Several of the women have expressed a desire to attend a Bible study that will teach them how to be dynamic, obedient Christians; to establish priorities and to be godly wives, mothers, and effective witnesses. Lois has a similar burden and would like to teach such a group.

Last week a group of women came to her and asked if she would start such a study, in her home if necessary. Her husband is on one of the ruling boards in the church and likes the idea but has warned her not to offend or in any way undermine the official study group. If you were Lois, how would you creatively instigate?

1. One definition of creative instigation is doing innovative things in a nonthreatening way. List as many ways as you can of how Lois could start such a group without offending the present teacher or attacking the present structure.

_____
_____
_____

GROWING, SHARING, SERVING

2. Alternative thinking is a part of creative instigation. List as many alternatives as you can to the problem Lois is facing. What could she do besides starting a home Bible study?

_____
_____
_____
_____

3. When you creatively instigate, you should have good, valid reasons for why you want to change something. List several reasons Lois could share as to why the present Bible study should be modified or an alternative offered.

_____
_____
_____
_____

4. Another aspect of creative instigation is to work within the existing structure. State some ways Lois and the women who want a different kind of study could feed into the existing Bible study and change it without starting a new group.

_____
_____
_____
_____

5. To creatively instigate, Lois must work through existing channels so she does not jump the chain of command. Put the following list of positions in the order you would use to approach the people who are involved. Cross out any you think should not be contacted or that would not apply. Add any you think are missing. After

Creative Instigation

you have chosen the order, write a paragraph in which you say what you think Lois should say to each one when she talks with them.

pastor   Christian education director   Sunday School superintendent   president of women's group   present teacher of Bible study   pastor's wife   women from the existing group   prayer partner   Christian education board   other women in the congregation

_____
_____
_____
_____
_____
_____
_____
_____

6. Lois must know what she is doing if she wants to creatively instigate, and she must properly communicate with others about her goals. Write a response Lois might make to each of the statements or questions listed below.

a) A group of concerned women asks Lois to start and teach such a study group. Lois's reply:

_____
_____
_____

b) The present Bible study teacher phones Lois and says, "I understand you are thinking about starting another women's Bible study." Lois's reply:

_____
_____
_____

GROWING, SHARING, SERVING

c) The pastor says, "Mrs. Davidson has been a faithful member for years and taught that class when no one else would take it. She is a good teacher and counselor." Lois's reply:

_____
_____
_____

d) The Christian education director says, "Maybe we could have the class on Sunday morning rather than compete with Mrs. Davidson's Thursday group." Lois's reply:

_____
_____
_____

e) A woman from the existing group says, "Many of the women who want to start a new study have never attended the one we have now. They should try it before criticizing it, or before they try to start something else." Lois's reply:

_____
_____
_____

7. If you were Lois, how would you answer these two questions?
a) What is the major problem?

_____
_____
_____

b) What do we all really want to accomplish?

_____

_____

1. Arthur DeMoss and David Enlow, *How to Change Your World in 12 Weeks* (Old Tappan, N.J.: Revell, 1969), p. 30.

SUCCESSFUL STRATEGIES
8

By now you probably have a general idea about how you would like to minister, what your areas of giftedness are, and how to get going. Now, how can you gain momentum and get from where you are to where you want to be?

GOD'S FORMULA FOR SUCCESS

God has spelled out His secret for success in Joshua 1:8: "This book of the law shall not depart from your mouth, but you shall meditate on it day and night, so that you may be careful to do according to all that is written in it; for *then* you will make your way prosperous, and *then* you will have success" (emphasis mine). If you want a successful ministry, first you should meditate on the Word of God. In Hebrew the word *meditate* means to concentrate on and practice. In other words, you must incorporate biblical principles into your life and act according to Scripture.

Second, you should take care to obey the principles you meditate upon. You will do certain things and abstain from doing others. Psalm 1:1-2 says you will not walk in the counsel of the wicked, stand in the path of sinners, nor sit in the seat of scoffers. Rather, you will delight in God's law and meditate on it. Then, the psalmist says, you will prosper in whatever you undertake.

Sounds simple, doesn't it? But how closely do we follow God's success formula? If we would practice the methods He prescribes, no person, no circumstances, could keep us from doing God's will. *No one but you can hinder or thwart your purposes.*

Let me share an example. Many years ago I wrote a teacher-training course. We were members of a small church that badly needed teachers. So I took the methods I had learned in my secular education and applied them to the Christian setting. I could hardly wait to teach the course! The problem was, the church already had a teacher-training class that everyone was required to take. I had taken it before I started teaching my second-grade Sunday school class, even though I was a professional, credentialed teacher and it was outdated and not as comprehensive as it should have been.

I fought and struggled and finally won approval to teach my course one time: at 7:30 Sunday morning before regular Sunday school began. Needless to say, attendance was poor, and the Christian education board decided to keep the other course rather than using mine. I was brokenhearted. I could not understand why God had allowed me to put in all those hours writing a teacher-training course only to have it shoved aside.

Shortly after that, due to unrelated events, George and I moved our membership to another, larger church. One day I received a call from the pastor telling me that the woman who ran the children's division was leaving to get married. He wondered if I would take the position she was vacating. One of his greatest concerns was that because the church was going to have double services to accommodate the growing congregation, they would be forming duplicate Sunday schools, which meant they would need about three hundred teachers trained and ready to go into the classrooms in a three-month period.

My husband and I taught my "neglected" teacher-training course to over four hundred potential teachers, quite a few of whom are still teaching. And I discovered that my goals had not been thwarted or my success hindered, but that God had a specific plan for when and where I would use that material. Even today, I use a lot of the material from the course when I speak at seminars and conventions and do teacher-training workshops in various churches. God has amplified that particular phase of my ministry in numerous ways. He did not let any person or circumstances keep me from doing His will or achieving success.

I learned a valuable lesson from that experience. If I am determined to follow a course of action, and someone blocks what I am trying to do, or it conflicts with an existing program, or consent of the necessary parties is refused, it does not mean my idea was not good or that I was not supposed to do it. It can mean that I am in the wrong time frame or the wrong setting, and that God is

Successful Strategies

using these roadblocks to direct me down the successful path He has planned for me.

Proverbs 3:5-6 says, "Trust in the Lord with all you heart, and do not lean on your own understanding. In all your ways acknowledge Him, and He will make your paths straight." Based on my experience, I am convinced that God never blocks a road unless it is not His chosen way. He never hinders our progress; He sets up detours so He can cause *more* to happen, not less. He withholds little so He can give much.

To help you understand more about God's strategies for success, look up each passage and fill in the chart with the appropriate information.

	Condition for Success	Result
Jer. 17:7-8		
Psa. 23:1-3		
Psa. 34:10		
Psa. 37:23-25		
Psa. 84:11		
Psa. 92:12-15		
Psa. 119:1-2		
Prov. 1:22-23		
Prov. 11:3		
Prov. 11:18		
Prov. 13:20		
Prov. 14:23		
Prov. 16:3		
Prov. 18:12		
Prov. 28:20		

GROWING, SHARING, SERVING

You are the one who hinders your success when you force something at the wrong time, or for the wrong reasons, or in the wrong place, or when you give up too soon, or when you are disobedient to God's success formula. You accomplish what you want when you have enough faith in yourself and your sovereign God to keep on keeping on until you arrive at the perfect place and point in time that God has structured for you. Do not discard your goals and plans, but be ready to readjust your present ideas about how and when to do things.

TRY TRYING

Preconceived ideas can be deadly because they stifle creativity and keep you from exploring possibilities. They mold you into an "I can'ter." An "I can'ter" is someone whose automatic response to a request for help is, "Oh, I couldn't do that." Or she goes the conservative route and analyzes opportunities to death, then says, "It would never work." Generally an "I can'ter" is a person who does not want to be bothered with facts or challenges because she already has made up her mind.

Angela was an "I can'ter." She was in my Bible study group and was an extremely enthusiastic and capable young lady, but she limited herself because she had decided she wanted to counsel women in the area of marriage and family. The first time she approached me with the idea I told her I thought she was a bit too inexperienced and had not been a Christian long enough to do that sort of counseling. I suggested that she take a teacher-training course and try teaching a children's Sunday school for a few months so she could work with both children and parents and be exposed to their problems firsthand. Besides, I knew that with her personality she would be a natural with children.

"Oh, I can't," she answered quickly. When I asked her why not, she said, "Just because I could never teach Sunday school. I don't want to teach children. I would not be good at it." She had three preconceived ideas: she could not, she did not want to, and she would fail if she did.

Weeks passed, and Angela became more and more frustrated. She met a couple of women who were having domestic problems, so she invited each one to her home so she could advise them. One refused the invitation and was offended that someone as young as Angela had been so presumptuous. The other went but did not appreciate Angela's efforts.

When that happened, she went to several people and asked for their opinions: an older woman she respected, a pastor, her husband, and her best friend. Each one, without the others knowing it, suggested that if she wanted to properly prepare herself she might teach Sunday school for a while and take some counseling courses at a local Bible institute.

One day Angela came into my office, and without even saying hello first, she asked, "Have you been talking to people, telling them to tell me to teach Sunday school?" I assured her I hadn't, and when she told me what had happened, I laughed. Reluctantly, she decided to try teaching Sunday school. She is now teaching in a preschool department and recently told me, "I love it! Absolutely love it. I don't know why I thought I wouldn't like it." I happen to know that she also has an effective ministry with the mothers of the children in her class.

Angela found out that "I can't" closes doors but "I'll try" opens them. Like Angela, you have nothing to lose and a lot to gain if you will make it a rule to try any good opportunity that is offered to you if it is at all possible. "I can't" is negative. "I'll try" is neutral. Trying something does not mean you are making a lifetime commitment; you are just exploring the possibilities and finding out what God has in mind for you. *You will never know what you are missing if you do not try!*

Think of your immediate sphere of operation. What are some opportunities that are available to you that you have already refused with a big, preconceived "I can't"? List them here.

_____

_____

Now put a star by one you will try, just to see what you can learn from the experience.

NEEDS VS. WANTS

Along with having the preconceived idea that you cannot do certain things, you may also have set notions about what you think you need if you are going to minister in the style to which you would like to become accustomed. There are many things you might think you need that are really unnecessary. As you explore possibilities, you should try to separate wants from needs, because they certainly are not the same.

Necessities are essentials that cannot be eliminated; wants and desires can be modified or eliminated. Many times you can sacrifice what you want in order to reach a goal. Remember the case study at the end of chapter seven about Lois? Perhaps she and the other women wanted a nice, daytime Bible study at the church with Lois teaching, but the need was to have some kind of

Successful Strategies

group that would minister in practical areas. It did not have to be a daytime class taught by a specific teacher, held in a preordained place at a set time of the week.

Most of us are so spoiled and pampered that we say we need something when we actually don't. Consequently, we end up with a mile-long list of "must haves," and we mess up our priorities.

Jesus taught a lesson about separating wants from needs. He and His disciples had been traveling, and they stopped at one of His favorite places, the home of Mary and Martha. Scripture tells us that "Martha welcomed Him into her home" (Luke 10:38). As any good hostess would do, she began preparing a place for her guests to sleep and food for them to eat, but her sister, Mary, "was listening to the Lord's word, seated at His feet" (Luke 10:39).

Martha felt Mary was not doing her part, so she "came up to [Christ] and said, 'Lord, do You not care that my sister has left me to do all the serving alone? Then tell her to help me' " (Luke 10:40).

But the Lord did not tell Mary to help. Instead He taught Martha a lesson in priorities. He "said to her, 'Martha, Martha, you are worried and bothered about so many things; but only a few things are necessary, really only one: for Mary has chosen the good part, which shall not be taken away from her' " (Luke 10:41-42).

Jesus stressed two principles in His answer. First, that the most important, enduring, profitable thing any man or woman can do is to sit at His feet and receive instruction from Him. We have already discussed the importance of Bible study and meditating on His Word. That is our first priority. How can we serve Him if we do not consult with Him? The issue should not be how to find time to study and pray when we have so much to do, but how to find time to do all of the things we have to do after

GROWING, SHARING, SERVING

we have spent proper time in prayer and study.

The second principle is that only a few things are necessary. He wasn't telling Martha not to be hospitable or putting her down for being domestic, but He was saying that relationships are more valuable than possessions and that people should take precedence over the preparations we make for them. Most of us live in such profuse self-indulgence, we forget that only a few things are really necessary; and we lose the peace and joy of the Lord because we are selfishly worried and bothered about so many things.

If you can learn to aim toward doing what is necessary—what Christ labeled "the good part"—rather than having what you want or what you think will look good or impress people, you will have more time, be more effective, and have a ministry that gives meaning and richness to others.

Do you have your wants and needs so intermingled that you cannot distinguish between the two? Fill in the blanks and see how your priorities match up to the standard Christ established with Martha.

1. Read Luke 10:38-42. What was Martha's stated need?

_____

What was Mary's unstated need?

_____

Why do you think the Lord said Mary's was a need and Martha's was a want rather than a necessity at that point?

_____
_____
_____

2. List as many of your personal needs as you can,

Successful Strategies

remembering that necessities are essentials you cannot do without.

———

3. Now list some of your wants, remembering they are things that can be modified or eliminated entirely.

———

4. List as many needs in your ministry as you can.

———

5. Now list some wants you have imposed on your area of ministry that could be changed, modified, or eliminated so that the basic needs can be fulfilled sooner and more efficiently.

(For example, I once thought that I had to be a hired member of a church staff to do what I want to do. I found that was a want, not a necessity, because my ministry functions as well and is growing since I have been working from an office out of my home. The need was that I prepare educational and study materials, write books, and teach Bible classes. I superimposed my wants onto my needs by deciding my base of operation had to be a church office, and in doing so, I got involved in many sideline issues that detracted from rather than lending to my basic goals.)

———

6. List the names of every person you have spent time with in the past twenty-four hours. Record one thing that happened when you were with that person; then

GROWING, SHARING, SERVING

check the appropriate column on the chart. Two examples are done for you.

Name	Type of Encounter	What was Accomplished	Meeting was a Need	Want
Brian (son)	Morning Devotions	Prayer, Bible Study, talked about the day	X	X
Neighbor	Talking in front yard	Gossiped about someone		X

Which of your encounters with people were necessary and valuable?

_____
_____

7. List every project you have spent time on in the past twenty-four hours. Then check the appropriate column on the chart.

Project	Time Spent	What Was Accomplished	Project Was a Need	Want

Are you devoting more time to things or people, to your own needs or the needs of others?

ENCOURAGING ENCOUNTERS

Another strategy God uses to build success and shake us loose from preconceived ideas is to show us His will through other people. This keeps us from being self-centered and prideful. Most of us are poor listeners, yours truly included, but the more miles I walk with the Master, the more I am convinced that He communicates with us through the people He sends into our lives.

For instance, I wanted to be a writer from the time I was eight years old. I worked on the school yearbook, wrote for the high-school paper, majored in English in college, read hundreds of books, and took a special two-year writing course by correspondence after I was married. But I always said the one thing I would never do was write a book. (Preconceived idea! Bad one!)

GROWING, SHARING, SERVING

As I taught my Bible study, one particular series of lessons about time management and self-discipline struck a deep chord with the women in the group. Irene came to me and said, "You have to put this into a book." As a matter of fact, Irene must have told me that at least a dozen times.

I shook my head and said, "I don't want to write a book."

Then Dolores and Emarie cornered me and told me they felt I should write a book based on the study series. "I'm too busy," I alibied, "and besides, I don't have a typewriter."

"Oh, don't worry about that," Emarie chirped. "You write it, and we'll see that it gets typed."

I was honestly disturbed, because I did not want to write that book. When I discussed it with Nancy, she jokingly said, "Well, think of it as a series of articles, since you are determined to write articles." She may have been teasing, but for the first time I gave serious consideration to the idea. I was almost afraid not to do it, because I was convinced that God had spoken to me through those dear friends.

Shortly after that, the field editor for a major book publisher phoned (I had never met the man) and asked if I might help get some women from my Bible study to attend a television taping at which one of his company's authors was appearing as a guest. He wanted some Christian women in the audience. Since it seemed that God had almost dropped him into my lap, I discussed the possibility of the book with him and asked what he thought of the topic. He said he would like to see my material and to send it to him when I had time.

That did it! No one sells a book that way, but I did. And I would still be writing articles if I had not finally listened to God's message He sent to me through His servants.

Successful Strategies

Now I am outlining my fifth book.

I have learned to view every encounter as a godly encouragement. God is sovereign. When we belong to Him, nothing happens by chance. Psalm 31:14-15 says, "But as for me, I trust in Thee, O Lord. I say, 'Thou art my God.' My times are in Thy hand." He can use everyone we meet, every event that transpires to contribute to our growth and development in a positive way. We need to learn to put up our antennae and ask ourselves, "What does God have in this for me?"

One way to enhance a godly encounter is to ask questions and solicit opinions. I frequently test my pet theories on pastors I meet by asking them if they feel an idea or interpretation is valid. A good question to ask is "What would you do if you were me?"

Each book I have written, each new step I take in my ministry, most of the possibilities I explore, have come to me through godly encounters. Even casual remarks or simple questions can give insight and direction. I have learned to listen when someone says, "Have you ever thought of writing a book about . . . ?" I am not saying I let others control my life or that I act on every word spoken to me, but I try to be continually sensitive to the fact that the Lord communicates with us through others.

Recently my dear friend Pauline asked if I had ever considered establishing a center to which women from different churches throughout the United States could come and be trained by a qualified staff about how to develop their personal spiritual potential and set up women's ministries in their home churches. The idea is so overwhelming that I did not even absorb it at first. But she kept talking about the possibilities and mentioning women she thought could help teach in it. She pointed out needs she felt could be met by such a center and asked the opinions of other Christian men and women.

GROWING, SHARING, SERVING

I have finally accepted the fact that God is telling me something through Pauline; but I am still so awed by the immensity of the concept that I cannot fully accept that He is already bringing it to pass. However, He is. There is no doubt that God uses others to direct your life!

Think about the conversations you have had with various individuals over the last ten days. Write down the statements they have made to you or questions they asked that could have been directional. (Be sure to include criticisms. I could write an entire book on how God has shown me my faults and failings through others.) If you cannot remember any, perhaps you need to sharpen your listening skills.

_____
_____
_____
_____

Remember, every encounter is a godly encouragement if you will accept it as such.

WORKSHOP

Here is your opportunity to evaluate yourself in the areas discussed in this chapter. Be as honest as you can. After each item on the following list, write the word that is most accurate for you: always, usually, sometimes, seldom, never.

1. I practice God's formula for success in my everyday life. _____

Successful Strategies

2. I am willing to accept the responsibility for my own failures. _____

3. I have many preconceived ideas. _____

4. Once I make up my mind, I do not readily change it.
_____

5. I am an "I can'ter." _____

6. I am optimistic. _____

7. I would rather not do anything than do what I do not want or like to do. _____

8. I focus on the needs of others more than I do on my own. _____

9. I focus on wants more than on the necessities. ___

10. My first priority is an active devotion to the Lord.

11. I will compromise if it will help a situation. _____

12. I am oriented more toward people than projects. _
_____

13. I am a good listener. _____

14. I accept negative criticism well. _____

15. I solicit the advice of others. _____

PERFORMANCE STANDARDS
9

SOMEONE ONCE SAID, "We search too high for things close by." How true! Sometimes we miss the chance to bring happiness or to do something that really matters because we have our heads in the clouds or are looking for the pot of gold at the end of the rainbow when we should be capitalizing on the reality of the moment.

Christ spoke of ministering a cup of water, walking an extra mile with a brother, and giving to those who are in need. He saw hungry people and fed them, lonely and hurting people and had compassion on them, sick people and healed them. He tried to show us that no ministry, regardless of how noticed or lauded it is, is any better than the sum of its parts. By example He set performance standards for us to follow. Let's look at four such standards that are necessary components for a successful life and ministry.

ON YOUR MARK, GET SET, GO!

The world has brainwashed us into believing that lowliness is the equivalent of failure. Christians who accept that misconception think they must work themselves into a position of rank or authority before they can minister to the fullest. But the Bible says that "God is not one to show partiality" (Acts 10:34). Jesus Christ said, "Whoever wishes to become great among you shall be your servant, and whoever wishes to be first among you shall be your slave; just as the Son of Man did not come to be served, but to serve, and to give His life a ransom for many" (Matt. 20:26-28).

If you want to do something, don't wait to be elevated to a higher position or for ideal circumstances; start where you are. Whatever God has for you to do does not lie ten miles down the road or in the nebulous future; it is facing you right now. No matter who you are, what you do, how much formal education you have, or what your background is, God wants you to serve Him where He has placed you at this very moment.

The apostle Paul is a good example for us. Although he was revered by many Christians and was chosen by God to carry the gospel to the Gentiles and to establish churches, after his conversion he spent more time in prison than he did in the synagogue. He never bemoaned his fate. He simply ministered wherever he was and could have cared less about his title or position.

GROWING, SHARING, SERVING

He shared the secret of his effectiveness when he wrote, "I have learned to be content in whatever circumstances I am. I know how to get along with humble means, and I also know how to live in prosperity; in any and every circumstance I have learned the secret of being filled and going hungry, both of having abundance and suffering need. I can do all things through Him who strengthens me" (Phil. 4:11-13). Paul is saying it doesn't matter what our position is or what our material circumstances may be. All that matters is that we minister where we are, assured that Jesus Christ will give us the strength to do it.

Do you practice servanthood? Are you making the most of each opportunity to minister? If you are, your ministry, as well as your interpersonal relationships, will flourish. If not, you probably feel like you are on a treadmill, trying to advance, using a lot of energy, but getting nowhere fast. Start where you are! That is God's beginning for you.

To help you see possibilities for ministries in your present setting, fill in the chart on the next page. After you have acted on the suggestions you make, put a checkmark by the line. (You may want to review the chart once a week to make sure you are making the most of the opportunities God sends your way.) An example is done for you.

DO THE WORST FIRST

Since we all tend to slight what we dislike doing and invest the most effort in what pleases us, we will accomplish more if we learn to do the worst first. Even in

Performance Standards

Name of Person	Relationship to Person	Need of Person	Ministering Possibility
Joanie	Gym Instructor	Separating from husband	Tell her I'll pray. Give her a Christian book with an encouraging message.

roles we love and ministries we enjoy there will be some things we find distasteful. If we eliminate them first, we can savor what is left.

Paul is also an example to us in this. No one thinks of him as a tentmaker, and he refers to himself as the apostle Paul, not the tentmaker Paul, but he did make his living making tents. He was no doubt consumed with the desire to teach the word and disciple early church leaders, but he told the Thessalonians, "Nor did we eat anyone's bread without paying for it, but with labor and hardship we kept working night and day so that we might not be a burden to any of you" (2 Thess. 3:8).

Paul did the worst first so he could devote the majority of his time to what he loved doing: preaching the gospel. A woman must be sure her home and family are in good order before she tackles ministries outside her home.

If we are going to have productive ministries, they must balance with the other activities in our lives. We cannot devote full time to any one thing. If all I did was research and write books, who would drive in the car pool, grocery-shop, serve in the snack bar at the Little

GROWING, SHARING, SERVING

League field, console a friend who calls, or run an errand for my husband? If we do only what we want to do or what appeals to us at the moment, we will never establish our priorities, and we will not be effective in anything we do.

Sometimes we are not aware that we put off doing things because we dislike them. Filling in the chart below may provide some perspective on this problem.

Tasks I Put Off Doing	One Reason Why	Time Required to Do Task	My Attitude Toward the Task

THINK SMALL

I recently read about a huge country-western music concert that was billed as the biggest extravaganza ever—the first of its kind—and featured dozens of famous stars. Original reports said 60,000 people would attend. But only 20,000 showed up. The producer told an interviewer he could not understand what had happened. I think I can. He didn't think small. He tried to do too much too soon.

Performance Standards

I want to stress that I am not saying don't dream big dreams or plan great plans. I am suggesting, however, that when it's time to implement those plans, you proceed slowly, cautiously, and modestly. No one starts at the top. You have to work your way up the ladder.

In a ministry, nothing that needs to be done to make it effective is meaningless or mundane. Every little thing matters to someone. A willingness to do so-called irrelevant tasks will open possibilities for larger service. We must approach our ministries with an attitude of humility, realizing there is nothing too menial for us personally to do.

Part of thinking small is attending to details, because they can make or break a project. For example, I have helped plan and organize dozens of women's retreats, and I have learned that proper rooming arrangements can spell success. When I took the time to be sure that each woman had the room partner of her choice, or that those who did not have a preference were put with women who would be compatible in age and interest, the retreat was more likely to be successful. The facility could be lacking, the food less than tasty, and the speaker could blow her talk, but if the women were happy with their roommates, they seemed to be able to adapt to other upsets.

Another part of thinking small is learning to underestimate rather than overestimate. If you are planning to hold an all-day women's seminar at your church, don't expect every woman in the congregation to come and bring three guests. Set the room up to accommodate a low, reasonable number. If more come, that's great, but don't plan to overwhelm the world; just try to reach a small, interested group.

Recently two large churches were planning retreats for their women. One advertised that there were only 75 openings and that reservations would be on a first come, first serve basis. The other announced that it had reserved 150 places and that women who wished to go could sign up for the next five weeks. Guess which church had the largest group at the retreat? The one that was limited to 75 places had to call and get extra reservations three times; they ended up with 128 women. The one that "thought big" had to cancel 40 beds.

A beautiful example of the right kind of thinking small is seen in the parable of the talents. The slaves who had been given five and two talents used them and doubled their original investments. And when their master saw that they had made the most of what he had given them, he commended them, saying, "Well done, good and faithful slave; you were faithful with a few things, I will put you in charge of many things" (Matt. 25:23). That's God's economy. Start out small, attend to the details, and He will put you in charge of more. Conversely, if you cannot handle a small job, you certainly can't handle a big one.

Remember, quality matters more than quantity. If you think small and are faithful with a few things, God will open up larger possibilities.

GOALS GET YOU THERE

Since the purpose of possibility exploration is to get you from where you are to where you want to be, the concept naturally includes setting goals for yourself and your ministry. Simply stated, a goal is a guideline, something you set for yourself to do, an achievement to strive for, a destination to reach. Setting goals helps you see

Performance Standards

where you have been and where you are going.

There are both long-range and short-range goals. Short-range goals are the stairsteps to reaching long-range ones. For example, if you want to become chairman of the missionary fellowship, you will need to set many short-range goals to help you work into the position. You might talk with the present and past chairpersons and ask them questions about what they did that was successful. You could serve in the group in other, lesser positions and correspond with some of the missionaries from the church.

Goals help you work up to your potential as well as giving direction; they act as roadmaps. For instance, our family decided to go on a lovely, month-long vacation last year. We planned to drive from Los Angeles to Chicago, along the Great Lakes to Maine, down the East Coast through New York City and Washington, D.C., and back through the Midwest to California.

The first thing we did when we decided to take the trip was to go to the auto club and have them chart our course so we would be sure to see everything we wanted to see and do all we hoped to do in the allotted time. If we had left home with no maps, eventually we would have reached the various destinations, but we would have wasted time and fuel driving around trying to find our way, and we would not have been able to see all of the sights.

Goals work like those maps. If we do not have any, we may possibly accomplish what we want, but we will waste time and effort trying to find our way. If we have a charted course of action, even some detours will not lead us astray. Goals give us direction and keep us centered on what we ultimately want to achieve.

Several years ago I set a long-range goal to do whatever I could to help further the concept of women's

GROWING, SHARING, SERVING

ministries. Since then I have taught numerous classes and seminars on the topic, shared my hopes, dreams, and ideas with pastors and women in many churches, and served as director of women's ministries on a church staff, during which time God allowed me to practice my theories. I am now writing this book in the hope that many of you will catch the vision and encourage this idea to develop in your churches.

Although my many short-range goals vary from day to day, my long-range goal is still the same. Knowing that it exists gives me the determination to keep on going, even when I get tired and discouraged.

Setting goals for yourself (or, if you have done that already, reviewing them on paper) could be productive. As you fill in the blanks below, remember that goals change as your circumstances vary and as you grow as a person. That means you will need to reassess your objectives frequently, deleting ones you have reached or eliminated and adding others as God shows you more possibilities.

1. List one long-range goal concerning your personal life.

_____

2. List three short-range goals you are implementing to help you reach the long-range one.

_____

_____

3. List one long-range goal concerning your ministry.

_____

_____

_____

Performance Standards

4. List three short-range goals you are implementing to help you reach the long-range one.

_____
_____
_____

WORKSHOP

List one performance standard for each of these verses. Then write how you can use that standard in your own ministry.

Matt. 5:43-44 Standard _____
My performance _____
Gal. 5:6 Standard _____
My performance _____
Eph. 5:1 Standard _____
My performance _____
Eph. 5:18 Standard _____
My performance _____
Phil. 1:27 Standard _____
My performance _____
Phil. 2:3-4 Standard _____
My performance _____
Rom. 12:3 Standard _____
My performance _____
Phil. 4:6 Standard _____
My performance _____

GROWING, SHARING, SERVING

Phil. 4:8 Standard _____
My performance _____
Col. 2:8 Standard _____
My performance _____
1 Thess. 4:11 Standard _____
My performance _____
2 Tim. 2:15 Standard _____
My performance _____
James 1:22 Standard _____
My performance _____
1 Pet. 3:8-9 Standard _____
My performance _____
1 Pet. 4:8 Standard _____
My performance _____
1 Pet. 4:10 Standard _____
My performance _____

PERSON-TO-PERSON SHARING
10

A WOMEN'S MINISTRY is not a program; it is a service provided to channel women in the way God leads. And no matter how large or small your church is, it should have either a woman or a committee to coordinate and direct the ministry, to oversee its operation and constructively pull loose ends together. The leader should be a resource person for the women of the congregation, someone they can come to with their ideas and problems. If your church uses a committee of women to head the ministry, its function would be the same but the duties could be subdivided.

GROWING, SHARING, SERVING
LEADERSHIP QUALITIES

The woman God appoints to help direct the women's ministry needs to have certain qualifications. She should be well-versed in the Word of God, because she will be involved in a spiritual ministry. She should be able to channel discussions and listen open-mindedly to opinions but stick to biblical ideas for answers. She should be wise and experienced enough to counsel women in problem areas.

She should also be able to <u>organize</u>, <u>administrate</u>, and <u>motivate</u> others. She should be a proven, faithful member of her local church and be confident enough of herself to take criticism. Above all, she should be a godly woman in her own walk and should have a humble, submissive spirit.

If a council is set up to direct the ministry, each member should meet whatever qualifications would be necessary for her to work effectively in her area of responsibility.

FUNDAMENTALS

Your church probably already has the foundation for a women's ministry. Almost every church has some kind of women's Bible study group, missionary organization, prayer group, or Sunday school class. And existing groups, no matter what their function is, should be looked upon as the foundation for the women's ministry. Rather than undermining or removing an ongoing, successful ministry, use it as the basis from which to expand into the other areas we will discuss. Such groups usually have leaders. That is a plus, because proper leadership is crucial to getting a women's ministry going and those in leadership positions have talents that can be used effectively.

Also, because of its many dimensions, a women's ministry needs a spiritual focal point, one from which all other activities and services spring. I am convinced that this hub should be a weekly Bible study, because it will keep the ministry centered and grounded in the Word. The study becomes a core group in which all of the women in the church can assemble to pray, fellowship, learn from and with one another, plan for the future, and evaluate ongoing ministries. In this group, age and role barriers are bypassed and the women are taught, discipled, and then sent out to minister in the other areas we have discussed.

DEACONESSES

Many churches have deaconesses. These women are usually elected by the congregation and are involved in a service ministry, primarily for the members of the church. They are selected based on the qualifications listed in Proverbs 31:10-31, 1 Timothy 3:8-13, and Titus 2:3-5. Many theologians believe the office of deaconesses was well established in the early church. The apostle Paul notes them by name in some of the epistles (for example, Rom. 16:1).

In an article titled "Deaconesses: Qualifications and Ministry," Ginger Moore Sper observes, "There is a need for these women workers in the church today just as there was a need for them then. Their ministries are varied because they have varied abilities for service, especially in the area of supplying the necessities of life, such as visiting those who are sick, teaching, praying, and showing hospitality. The ministrations of these women are based on similar ministries of women during Christ's life."

As for the qualifications of a deaconess, Mrs. Sper says, "Deaconesses are faithful stewards of God's work. Their faith is not superficial, and their actions speak for themselves. They are to teach the gospel of Christ and live it. They are trusted servants of God and man. Their purpose is to continually give themselves in meeting the needs of the church or its people. A deaconess's qualities are those of a virtuous woman. She is trustworthy, strong, and fears the Lord above all."[1]

Some of the areas in which deaconesses commonly serve in the modern church include:

- *Communion.* Preparing communion and cleaning up after the service. Maintaining linen, chrome and silver, in addition to purchasing the elements for the service.
- *Baptism.* Meeting with women candidates, assisting during the baptism service, and doing follow-up counseling.
- *Funerals.* Providing food and doing errands for families during the period of bereavement. Seeing that flowers are sent by the church.
- *Sickness.* Doing hospital visitation, chauffeuring people to and from the doctor, and caring for shut-ins—both at home and in convalescent facilities.
- *Needy.* Furnishing groceries and supplying clothes, toys, and birthday and holiday gifts for children. Helping families find lodging and assisting them when they move.
- *Miscellaneous services.* Supplying refreshments for

Person-to-Person Sharing

certain church functions, helping with receptions, weddings, preparing food for workdays and ministering to shut-ins by visiting, taking in food, reading to them, and praying with them.

• *Hospitality.* Opening their homes to church groups for meetings or socials and also offering lodging to people who have immediate needs.

This is not to say that women who are not elected nor formally titled deaconesses should not be involved in similar ministries, but these tasks seem to be commonly designated to women in churches who hold the office of deaconess.

NITTY-GRITTY MINISTRIES

Now let's look at the multitude of available opportunities. Again, let me stress that each of these ministries is operating in some form in one or more churches. They are all feasible, biblical, and they meet needs in the lives of women today. Women who have seen needs and taken the initiative to perform services to meet those needs are continually implementing new ideas. Many of these ministries were not founded or developed in the literal sense. They happened when God brought two people together, and they grew when others saw their usefulness.

I have divided the service opportunities into five basic categories because some churches prefer to develop each area under the direction of a separate leader or committee. Also, the categories broadly define the type of ministries listed under the heading. These divisions are not meant to be rigid or restrictive in any way but to make it

GROWING, SHARING, SERVING

easier to assess what is available and what needs are not presently being met.

- *Little Sister Program.* In the Little Sister Program, college and career age single girls are assigned to junior-high girls to be friends and spiritual counselors. This is done with parental approval. The Big Sister must be willing to spend quality time with her Little Sister, taking her shopping, going to sporting events, having her to her home for dinner, and remembering her birthday and other special occasions.

In some churches, the Big Sisters sponsor a social of some kind every two or three months, such as a swim party, slumber party, ice cream feed, or trip to the zoo or local amusement park. Two of the side benefits of this program are that it gives the single girls an opportunity to have contact with a family, and many parents have told me that the Big Sister has been an undergirding support to the values they are trying to teach their daughters. One mother said, "It's one thing when I tell Sandie not to do something, but when her Big Sister upholds what I say, she accepts it much more readily."

To get this ministry started, all you need are some single girls who are willing to become Big Sisters. There always seem to be plenty of junior highers who want to be assigned.

- *Widows' Ministry.* Scripture tells us to "honor widows who are widows indeed" (1 Tim. 5:3). But many churches inadvertently push widows aside because of today's great emphasis on family ministries. When this happens, we are wasting one of the most valuable resources in the Body of Christ. Widows are some of the most eligible, qualified women in the church; therefore, we should not only minister to them but use them to minister to others.

My friend Millie found this out a few years ago when

she was appointed deaconess in charge of the widows in her church. She said she was troubled, because she had no idea how to minister to them. She prayed and prayed; then one day, as she was reading the Bible, she came across the verse in Titus that says older women are to teach the younger ones. She was so excited she could hardly contain her enthusiasm. What other group of women would be as well trained and equipped, plus have the time, to minister to the needs of the younger women in the church? So rather than set up a ministry for poor, helpless, lonely widows, Millie instigated a ministry *by* the widows, based on a biblical principle she had learned.

Some ministries I have personally observed widows performing in various churches are teaching Sunday school and/or Bible studies, running the nursery facility, teaching practical arts such as quilting, crocheting, knitting, bread baking, jelly making, and home gardening—almost lost arts to many of the younger generation. Widows also serve on boards, act as surrogate mothers and grandmothers to younger women, and do family counseling.

Another perspective of this ministry is that of widows ministering to widows. When my father-in-law died, I saw what an alarmingly confusing mass of paperwork and bureaucratic entanglements my mother-in-law had to face at a time when she was emotionally vulnerable and least capable of thinking clearly. I was so bothered by the complexity of the situation that I discussed it with my friend Lillian.

Although her husband was still living at the time, he was gravely ill, and she knew he did not have long to live. I asked her if she had any idea of what she would need to do if Vern passed away before she did. She said she did not. So I asked her if she thought the women's ministry could set up a reference file for widows.

Lillian liked the idea, so she consulted a Christian attorney, then set up a file containing papers and forms that would need to be filed, addresses and phone numbers of agencies and names of people to call for information. When her husband died, she unselfishly kept a record of everything she had to do and developed a packet containing suggestions on how to handle the multitude of details that bombard a widow during the bereavement period.

Now when a woman in Lillian's church loses her husband, she is not only given condolences but practical assistance by a concerned Christian widow who knows the ropes. That is an example of widows ministering to widows.

A final benefit from a widows' ministry is that of mutual encouragement. It brings newly widowed women in contact with those who have lived through their loss and are learning to survive. It also develops a great basis for fellowship and prayer.

- *Singles.* It would be pretentious of me to try to enumerate the many needs or types of single women in our churches. College girls are singles, as are many career women, middle-aged divorcees, and elderly widows. In a women's ministry the thrust must be to integrate singles into the overall picture and overlap age barriers, rather than to segregate them, as is so frequently done.

Many churches fail to recognize the tremendous resource they have in their single women. The apostle Paul saw and stressed the value of singleness when he said, "The woman who is unmarried . . . is concerned about the things of the Lord, that she may be holy both in body and spirit; but one who is married is concerned about the things of the world, how she may please her husband" (1

Person-to-Person Sharing

Cor. 7:34). Paul is not delivering an indictment against marriage but exalting the pleasures of singleness.

The single women in the church have the freedom to devote both mind and body to the things of the Lord. A single girl doesn't have to miss teaching her Sunday school class on Sunday morning because her child wakes up sick. She can take a phone call from a distraught friend at two A.M. without worrying about waking her husband or family. She can stay after Bible study and pray as long as the Spirit leads, because she does not have to get home before school lets out. She can use her home in whatever way she and the Lord choose, without having to consider the schedules or moods of her husband and children. A women's ministry should use the single women to the fullest. They are a definite asset and can minister in ways married women cannot.

- *Mother-Child Relationships.* For years I have been aware that churches do not teach the practicalities of homemaking and motherhood. They teach theology but not how to practice it, so Bible study groups and Sunday school classes are filled with women and girls who feel inadequate in or do not understand their God-given roles. The older women have failed to teach the younger ones how to "love their husbands, to love their children . . . and to be workers at home" (Titus 2:4-5).

Ministries to mothers and homemakers should ideally cover three general categories: girls who are not married, young married women with or without children, and older married women with older children. Training unmarried girls how to be wives and mothers before they marry and bear children would alleviate many of the problems these youngsters face. Girls used to learn these things in their homes, but in today's society this simply is not done. The women's ministry can help compensate for this lack of training in several ways.

GROWING, SHARING, SERVING

It can minister to unmarried girls by sponsoring panel discussions about topics of interest to both mothers and daughters. It can offer practical-arts workshops and classes that teach biblical principles on the role of wife and mother to girls from junior-high age on, so their romantic notions about love and marriage are balanced with the duties and responsibilities that are involved.

Teenagers should be encouraged to serve in the church nursery so they can experience being with infants and toddlers and see firsthand just how much time and patience are involved in being a mother. I believe that the younger women referred to in Titus 2:3-5 are not necessarily married ones. I think the passage means that from childhood, girls should be taught how to become loving wives and mothers, so that if they marry and have children, they will be well equipped for the task at hand.

Ministries to young married women and mothers can teach both biblical principles and practical application, centering on discipleship by example. And the women's ministry should also have classes and counseling for older women who feel they are deficient in some way as mothers, wives, or homemakers. Women who have happy marriages and well-adjusted children should be willing to share their know-how with those who are less fortunate.

• *Counseling*. The women of a church can take personal, individual responsibility for the other women in their midst. Most churches do not have trained, professional counselors, but all have women who have had problems and, by the grace of God, have learned how to cope and conquer. This phase of a women's ministry needs women who are willing to share their victories with those who are trapped in similar problems.

Some problem areas in which counseling expertise is needed include:

- *Alcohol.* Counseling for women who are drinkers or who have husbands or children who drink. Some training in Al-Anon is helpful.
- *Drugs.* Counseling for women who misuse drugs or who have family members or friends who do.
- *Abuse.* Counseling for women who are battered or whose children are being emotionally or physically abused.
- *Juvenile problems.* Counseling for mothers of older children who are having emotional or behavior problems.
- *Unequally yoked partners.* Counseling for Christian women who are married to unbelievers.
- *Social issues.* Counseling to help women sort through pertinent issues, such as women's liberation, ERA, divorce, abortion, and employment problems.
- *Communication.* Counseling in techniques that will help build understanding and openness, especially within a family.
- *Divorce.* Counseling on biblical principles as well as the unique types of problems faced by divorcees, such as single parenthood, loss of self-esteem, and depression.

All of these are person-to-person ministries that put women directly in touch with other women so they can encourage, exhort, and edify one another in the love of Christ. What do you think God would have you do?

WORKSHOP

Which of the person-to-person ministries discussed in this chapter are operational in your church?

GROWING, SHARING, SERVING

List at least six needs you know of, in your own life or the lives of your friends and acquaintances, that could be met by some of the ministries discussed in this chapter.

_____

_____

_____

_____

_____

From the list of the person-to-person ministries, list one area in which you feel you could serve effectively.
_____

Write the names of three women you know who could contribute in some way to one or more of the person-to-person ministries.

1. _____
2. _____
3. _____

Would you be willing to tell each woman about the possibilities you see for her? Make an appointment with each of them.

---

1. Ginger Moore Sper, "Deaconesses: Qualifications and Ministry" (unpublished paper).

CHALLENGES IN SERVING
11

BOOKER T. WASHINGTON SAID, "No race can prosper until it learns that there is as much dignity in tilling a field as there is in writing a poem." I would like to paraphrase that and say, "Our families will not prosper until every woman learns that there is as much dignity in being a wife, mother, and homemaker as there is in a worldly career." And, if Christian women are going to devote themselves first and foremost to caring for their husbands and children, as Scripture teaches they should, they need to be trained in the domestic arts. A women's ministry should offer guidelines and instruction on the how-to's of everyday living.

GROWING, SHARING, SERVING

SERVICE OPPORTUNITIES: PRACTICAL MINISTRIES

God Himself laid the foundation for a practical-arts ministry by establishing a pattern for us in the verbal portrait of a godly woman in Proverbs 31:10-31. The Bible says that a woman who fears the Lord "works with her hands in delight. . . . She looks well to the ways of her household, and does not eat the bread of idleness" (Prov. 31:13, 27).

Churches have sometimes been so busy preaching "religion" that they have forgotten that we all need to be shown how to act out our theology. If a woman is going to conform to the pattern of the ideal God has placed in Scripture, she must be taught how to cook, sew, shop, and budget both her time and money. That is the purpose of the practical-arts part of a women's ministry.

GENERAL SKILLS

Homemaking and motherhood are careers in which a woman can excel, find deep satisfaction, be noticed, and gain positive recognition. Yet, many females fail in their roles as wives and mothers, because they have not been taught or trained how to perform or enjoy what they are doing. A women's ministry can supplement deficiencies in domestic training by providing classes in sewing, knitting, crocheting, needlepoint, home decorating, budgeting, food preparation, and the other skills that will help the Christian woman be a steward of her time and talents as outlined in Proverbs 31.

There is undoubtedly someone in your congregation

Challenges in Serving

who is already equipped to teach other women the how-to's of each of these areas. To start a practical-arts ministry, all you need to do is look for women who are skilled in certain areas and ask them to share their techniques with a group.

One church I know of has a Christmas club. In January, a group of women start making decorations, ornaments, wrapping paper, and gifts. They make three of each item; one to send to a missionary family, one to sell at a fund-raising boutique in November, and one to keep. The women in that club do not spend much money on store-bought Christmas items.

This week I am teaching a class for mothers whose children are attending daily vacation Bible school. The first half of the morning is a Bible class on the practicalities of Christianity and the woman's role. The second part is practical arts: we are making quilts for missionaries. Most of the women had never made a quilt, so they are learning how for their own use, too. Several of them are not saved. They are experiencing prayer, study, and fellowship for the first time and also learning something tangible they can use at home.

PERSONAL DEVELOPMENT

Another characteristic of a godly woman is that she "makes coverings for herself; her clothing is fine linen and purple. . . . Strength and dignity are her clothing" (Prov. 31:21, 25). She is well groomed and modest—not easy standards to live up to in today's fashion conscious, sex-oriented society.

Many young women in our churches come from

non-Christian homes and are grounded in worldly values. They have never been presented with God's views It is imperative that the church provide personal development courses for young girls, and women of all ages for that matter, because what they see and hear at school, on television, and in the world is so contrary to what the Bible teaches.

A personal development course should include such topics as attitude dimensions, charm, grooming and manners, personality assessment, figure classification, hairstyling, makeup, and voice modulation. Again, there are probably those in your local congregation who could teach these things. In several churches hairdressers and women who sell cosmetics do workshops on applying makeup and hair care. In a small Midwest community, the lady who owns the dress shop teaches a class on grooming and selecting a wardrobe. I know of a dentist's wife, who is also a hygienist, who does an eight-hour seminar on personal health and social graces.

An important part of any personal development program centers around diet and exercise. The Bible very clearly teaches that your body is the temple of the Holy Spirit, was purchased by God for His glory, and that intemperance toward food is a sin. Part of our witness to an unbelieving world is to be happy and healthy.

My friend Shirley was a bit overweight and did not feel very good about herself because she was, in her words, a disorganized and sloppy person. She decided she wanted to change, so she diligently learned self-discipline through studying Scripture, praying, and being discipled by a woman who is quite organized and efficient. She also took a course in nutrition offered as a community service at a local hospital. After that she corralled a physical education teacher and started teaching a course in diet, health, exercise, and self-discipline.

Challenges in Serving

Shirley is a radiant, self-controlled lady, and she has helped dozens of women in her church. She identified her Spirit-planted desire, developed her natural talents, and is ministering her gift of helps. All it takes to start any facet of a women's ministry is one dedicated woman like Shirley.

PRESCHOOL OBSERVATION

The godly woman in Proverbs 31 is undoubtedly a good mother because "her children rise up and bless her" (v. 28). Happy, whole, emotionally resilient children do not happen accidentally: they are the result of proper training, love, and understanding. Yet, for the most part, mothers of preschoolers concentrate on the physical needs of their children more than on the spiritual and emotional, probably because they are the most obvious. Many of them simply do not know how to "nurture" a child.

Delphine, a vivacious mother of four, came to me one day and shared that she was disturbed because she had been attending, with her young daughter, a preschool observation class held at a neighborhood school. The mothers were instructed to watch their children play and do projects. Then they would discuss how to handle the behavior they had observed. She said, "What bothers me is that what these women come up with is so contrary to Scripture. They really want to do what is best for their kids but they don't know how."

Delphine's concern was well founded. What she wanted to do was base a similar class at the church (after all, why not use the facility during the day once a week?)

but teach biblical principles of child-raising during the discussion time. It took a while, but that group meets once a week now, and God graciously sent a woman with a master's degree in early childhood education to help with the class. When I think of instances like this, in which one concerned woman like Delphine cared enough to step out in faith, I am reminded of my favorite quote by J. Hudson Taylor: "Depend on it! God's work done in God's way never lacks God's supply."

SERVICE OPPORTUNITIES: SERVICE MINISTRIES

Closely connected to the practical arts are what I call service ministries. Our model woman in Proverbs 31 "makes her arms strong.... She extends her hand to the poor; and she stretches out her hands to the needy" (vv. 17, 20). One of Christ's primary tasks was to serve others. That, He said, is why He came.

At the risk of sounding like a broken record, I want to again emphasize how necessary it is that the older women in the church help young mothers in any way possible. Raising children in today's world is different than it was when my babies were born twenty some years ago. Life is so intense now. These young women are pressured to be perfect—immediately.

The extended family is almost extinct. A few decades ago when a baby was born, there were aunts, cousins, grandparents, and parents to help share the load. That is not so now. Frequently young mothers are entirely alone, with no other woman to turn to for help and guidance. They do not know how to parent their children, and they are confused, frustrated, and frightened.

I believe the church should be willing to be an extended substitute family to these young women, to be the loving support system they need.

NURSERY NUGGETS

If hospitals offer courses in infant care, why shouldn't churches? I have been in several churches in which this is done, with the plus of providing foundational lessons in how to manifest the love of Christ to babies and toddlers.

In one church, the nursery superintendent teaches a weekly class that runs for four sessions for mothers of newborns. The woman who teaches the course is not a professional nurse, but she is one of those people who has a sense about children, a special God-given antenna of awareness. Not only does she teach the mothers how to physically care for their infants, but how to teach Bible verses to babies, pray for and with them, and sing songs to them.

The day I sat in on her class, she was answering questions that had been turned in at the previous session. One mother asked what she should do if her baby wouldn't sleep when he should. Nana laughed and said, "Oh, he'll sleep when he should. What you mean is, what should you do if he won't sleep when *you* want him to." She made her point.

Some churches have set up telephone hotlines for mothers of infants and toddlers, so if they have a problem or just get upset and frustrated with their children, they can call an objective, interested person and discuss how they feel and get suggestions about what to do. In one church, widowed grandmothers take most of the hotline calls. Some even make house calls, going into homes where more than advice or moral support is needed.

MOTHER'S DAY OUT

Many young mothers say they feel trapped in their environment when they have one or more preschoolers at home. Lissie said, "Sometimes I think I can't talk in words of more than one syllable." These feelings are intensified because most young couples cannot afford to pay a daytime sitter so the wife can go out. A number of churches are helping these young housewives and mothers by offering what they call "mother's day out."

Once or twice a week older women volunteers provide free child care at the church nursery. Most churches that do this have games and story time, plus organized and free play time for the preschoolers. The day usually begins at ten in the morning and runs until mid-afternoon. Mothers are asked to bring a sack lunch for their children; then they can have a free day to do whatever they wish, knowing that their little ones are well cared for.

TUTORING

In any church there are children who need extended help in basic learning skills. There are also men and women who can be trained to tutor elementary age children in reading, math, and language. Private tutors are expensive, and it is not good stewardship to make parents pay to get help for their boys and girls if the church can aid them without charge.

In churches that have tutoring service, a professional teacher, who is frequently a member of the congregation, trains volunteers in using materials and teaching basic skills. I know of one instance in which the public-school principal was so thrilled that a church wanted to help in this way that he personally instructed the aides who would be working with the children. Some churches charge a small fee to cover the cost of materials.

There are side benefits to a tutoring service. One woman met with the teacher of a girl she was helping and ended up leading her to Christ. The children's grades almost always improve and so does their behavior. Also, the tutors can teach biblical values and talk about the Lord with their students. Some churches use Christian literature for the reading portion of the tutorial program.

HELPS

The helps section of a women's ministry is for women who do not mind legwork. It is doing behind-the-scenes duty. Some types of services involved are:
- *Cleaning.* Helping maintain church facilities, beyond normal custodial care. One church has a crew of women who clean and sterilize the nursery every week and also do the laundry.
- *Paperwork.* Doing secretarial work, such as filing, collating, addressing envelopes, and keeping attendance records.
- *Transportation.* Driving elderly or disabled people or

GROWING, SHARING, SERVING

doing errands for them.
- *Food preparation.* Helping prepare food for church functions or church members.
- *Clothes and food storage.* Helping maintain and distribute goods that are donated to the church.
- *Community services.* Ministering to families in the neighborhood by offering support and material help when problems arise, such as burned homes, or death or illness in the family.

Christ challenged us to serve others in tangible, meaningful ways: feeding them, clothing them, giving them something to drink when they are thirsty, inviting them into our homes, and visiting those who are sick and in prison. He said, "to the extent that you did it to one of these brothers of Mine, even the least of them, you did it to Me" (Matt. 25:40). Are we meeting that challenge?

WORKSHOP

What are the practical-arts and service ministries that are presently operational in your church?

_____
_____
_____

What would you like to see started?

_____
_____
_____

Challenges in Serving

How could you contribute personally in each of the following areas?
- Personal development _____
- Domestic arts _____
- Preschool ministries _____
- Nursery ministries _____
- Tutoring _____
- Helps _____

If you are a younger woman, what are some of the ministries discussed in this chapter that you believe would meet a need in your life?

_____
_____
_____

What is at least one way you could help get such a ministry going? (Have you made your needs known? Is there an older woman you can talk to, who might disciple you or know what to do or who to contact?)

_____
_____
_____

SPIRITUAL DIMENSIONS
12

SEVERAL MONTHS AGO I spoke at the banquet of a women's auxiliary of a well-known Christian organization. One of the things I stressed, as I challenged the women to become actively involved in ministering to others, is that any work we do in the name of the Lord is a spiritual ministry. Afterwards, a young woman named Peggy came up to me and explained that she is a secretary for one of the auxiliary chapters. She said she has always felt that her "pencil pushing and phone calling" did not count for much.

"But," she bubbled, "hearing that my secretarial work is a spiritual ministry has given me a new perspective. I don't feel like a second-class Christian anymore!"

Spiritual Dimensions

All work done for the cause of Christ is a spiritual ministry, and that includes every possibility for service we have explored in this book. So this chapter title, "Spiritual Dimensions," does not imply something different from what has gone before. The following ministries are perhaps more overtly and obviously spiritual and are looked upon as foreground ministries in the church, which is geared first and foremost to teach the Bible, evangelize, and disciple. But by looking at the other types of ministries first, we could better explore new possibilities before coming to these.

BIBLE STUDIES

It is important for a women's ministry to have a central Bible study, but that core group should not be the only Bible study. Other classes should be developed as need arise. Some possibilities for grouping that I have found successful are groups for topical and book studies: groups of singles, divorcees, and single parents; young marrieds; young mothers; married women: women over thirty; and mother-daughter study groups.

There are also several ways to set up a Bible study group. Beyond the basic structure discussed in Titus 2:3-5, any Bible study class should include these biblical components: fellowship, including refreshments if you wish; study of God's Word; and prayer. This is in keeping with the pattern set by the early church in Acts 2:42.

Teaching methods depend upon the size and needs of the group and on the teacher herself. There are numerous ways to approach the format. A group can be taught by the leader/teacher with no discussion during the lesson but with questions and answers afterwards. The group can be led by a leader/teacher who presents a basic lesson but allows for questions and discussion to take place while she is teaching. Or, the study can be led by several group leaders, and the class can be broken down into smaller groups without any master teacher/leader. The danger here is that smaller groups can become introspective, and it is also difficult to find competent leaders.

The materials that are used will also depend on the needs of the group and teacher preference. There are many excellent study guides for women on today's market, or a leader may prefer lessons she prepares herself. One basic necessity in any format is the opportunity for *interaction* between the leader and the women in the group.

Prayer is a crucial part of the Bible study. Too often time that should be spent communicating with the Lord is spent giving requests. To avoid this, it is helpful to have prayer request sheets for the women to fill out. The woman writes her request and turns it in to the prayer leader. Then during prayer time her request is held before the Lord. In the Bible study I teach, I keep the request sheets with me for one week, praying daily for each one; the next week I review the request, note any updated information on the form, and give it to one of the women in the group to pray for until the prayer has been answered.

Prayer time also needs to include a time of sharing praises. I think it quenches the Spirit if the women have to write their praises on paper, so we have a time of spontaneous sharing of praises for answered prayer. Since many of the women have been praying for the requests that have been made, this is a great blessing to everyone in the group.

The method used for praying will also depend on the

Spiritual Dimensions

size and needs of the group. In large classes, it is best to have one person pray or to divide the group into small prayer cells and let them have conversational prayer. If a group is small, the women can pray as they are led, remembering the requests that have been given. If you choose to have conversational prayer, avoid going around the room or asking any specific person to open or close. Let the Lord dictate those matters.

Whether the study group is held at the church or in a home, for a study to run smoothly and minister effectively you will need to be well organized. Some basic necessities are:

- A baby sitter. If the study is held at the church or in a home, have the sitter elsewhere! Children who know mommy is in the next room are disruptive and won't rely on the sitter.
- Someone to buy supplies, such as coffee or juice, cups, and napkins.
- Someone to bring goodies. Try a rotating list.
- A secretary to keep a roster and to send greetings to first-time visitors.
- A prayer chairman to keep the request sheets and to set up a telephone prayer chain.
- A treasurer to handle funds for outreach ministries, to sell supplies, and to take an offering if your group wants to collect money for some reason.

EVANGELISM AND OUTREACH

Many times study groups tend to grow inward rather than outward. Everyone gets to know everyone else and a sort of Christian clique develops. This is a poor testimony and thwarts the basic purpose of the study group, which is for women who are in the Word of God to pass on what they are learning. Primary outreach functions of any Bible study should be to win others *to* Christ, disciple them *in* Christ, and to minister *through* Christ, in His name. We must apply the truths we learn. Paul cautioned that "knowledge makes arrogant, but love edifies" (1 Cor. 8:1). James extols us to be "doers of the word and not merely hearers" (James 1:22).

A Bible study should, therefore, include some kind of Christian service project and have a continual thrust toward starting other study/service groups. The leaders must never be satisfied with the status quo and should encourage members to find individual means of service as well as those within the group.

Some outreach projects that have been effective in Bible study groups are hospital service ministries, in which women from the group go into local hospitals or convalescent homes to read, talk, and pray with patients; juvenile hall outreach, in which women go into the local juvenile facility and take refreshments, books, records, and magazines, and talk to the young people there; and evangelism, in which the group sponsors some kind of witnessing activity, such as coffees, teas, or book reviews. Many of the practical arts and service ministries that were discussed earlier can be used for evangelism and outreach.

SPECIAL EVENTS

Another way the women's ministry can reach out is to sponsor special events. At a recent teachers' rally, the

Spiritual Dimensions

pastor said, "I know you've heard them say on television that 'we interrupt the regular programming to bring you this special event.' Well, that's what we're doing—interrupting our regular classes to bring you this special seminar."

These happenings can be presented for Christians and still be structured to attract unbelievers, so women can bring unsaved friends, neighbors, and relatives without having them suffocated in "religion." Outreach meetings should motivate Christians as well as whet the spiritual appetites of unbelievers and make them want to find out more about what they see and hear.

Some outreach events that have been effective include:

• *Panel discussions.* In my church we once had a panel discussion called, "To Bikini or Not To Bikini: That Is the Question." Actually, our topic was modesty, and each woman on the panel had a particular biblical point she was going to present; but many mothers and daughters (and a few boyfriends, too) had an opportunity to vent their feelings and ideas about beach attire. The women who moderated the panel made strong arguments from Scripture against immodest attitudes in today's society. I know of three girls who, with no prodding from their moms, got rid of their bikinis after the meeting.

• *Retreats.* My definition of a retreat is a "getaway." Too often we cram retreats so full of meetings and activities that women get on an emotional high rather than relaxing in God's peace. If a Christian woman invites an unbeliever, she will need time to talk with her, discuss what is being taught, and enjoy her company. All retreats should be getaways in which the women have a break in their regular routine and have time to rest and play as well as to meditate and contemplate.

• *Evangelistic seminars.* This churchwide event is geared so the women in the congregation can invite

GROWING, SHARING, SERVING

Program

10:00 A.M.	Welcome and Introductions
10:15	Keynote "Duplicating: Disciples and Disciplers"
11:15	FEMINARS (choose one) "Single" "Creative Counterpart" (wives) "Widows and Widowhood" "Let's Live" "Interior Decoration in the Christian Home"
12:30 P.M.	SALAD BUFFET & Style Show
2:00 P.M.	AFTERNOON FEMINARS (Choose a second class from the morning list)
3:30 P.M.	Adjourn

Spiritual Dimensions

One value of a feminar is that it gives many women in the church a chance to teach what they are best at. It also provides a way to minister in practical areas of a woman's life. Here are some especially clever and meaningful feminar topics. All of these were presented as workshops with an emphasis on audience involvement.

"Behave Yourself"	Principles of godly conduct from Proverbs
"Up N' At 'Em"	Biblical principles of self-discipline
"Clock Watching"	Principles of time management
"Be a Sew and Sew"	Basic sewing techniques
"Grandma Lives Here"	Coping with the physical and emotional problems of the elderly in the home
"Daring Discipleship"	Methods of how to work with someone on a one-on-one basis
"Godly Graces"	Personal development
"Mother Did It Wrong"	Biblical principles of child raising
"Healthy Is Happy"	Suggestions for women over forty about how they can maintain their health
"Don't Be Angry"	Biblical principles on proper use of emotions

outsiders to come and hear a speaker. The topic should be one of current interest to all women but needs to include the gospel as well.

The topic of one seminar we sponsored was self-image, which has relevance to women of all ages and status. Dr. Pamela Reeve, dean of women at Multnomah School of the Bible in Portland, Oregon, was the speaker. The event was publicized in newspapers, and letters were sent to other churches in the vicinity, inviting them to attend. After the seminar, refreshments were served, and many women had an opportunity to talk with Dr. Reeve and to share Christ with visitors.

- *Feminars.* A feminar is the female equivalent of a seminar. I have found that these are an extremely effective way to both evangelize and teach to meet the needs of women who are churched. The format can vary, but most feminars are a full day in length and include general meetings, in which instruction is given to all of the women who attend, plus several workshops, which run consecutively two or three times throughout the day.

To conduct a feminar, you need to pick a date, decide on the time, topics, and speakers. The next step is publicity. You will probably need to have some planning meetings. Your feminar can be as elaborate or simple as you wish. You should take advantage of the situation and publicize the ongoing Bible studies, ministries, and upcoming events. By asking the participants to fill out evaluation cards, you can get the names and addresses of those who came in addition to finding out what was effective and what wasn't.

SPIRITUAL DIMENSIONS

Once the women's ministry in your church starts growing, you will need some kind of system so all of the women who are involved can meet and communicate. You will also want to recruit new workers, and as new ministries develop you will need to promote and advertise them. All these goals can be accomplished at a semiannual women's leadership forum.

All of the women in the congregation are invited to the forum. Each lady who is leading a phase of the women's ministry should share what is happening in her particular ministry, what its spiritual and practical purposes are, and what opportunities there are for involvement. At the close of the forum, the following form is passed out. The women are asked to fill it in and are invited to attend a follow-up meeting so they can receive detailed information about their area of interest and discuss what they would like to do in the way of service.

DO A DREAM!

I hope the ideas and concepts in this book have inspired you to define your Spirit-planted desires, use your spiritual giftedness as never before, and become a ministering woman who will never settle for less than what God has for you. I hope you will pray with me for an awakening to service of Christian women everywhere so we can individually and collectively have a positive, godly effect on the entire world. And I pray that you will purpose in your heart to creatively instigate a women's

GROWING, SHARING, SERVING

ministry in your local church, or further develop the one that exists. Do a dream! God will make it come true.

WORKSHOP

Read each set of verses from Proverbs 31 and state in your own words what personal performance or attitude is expected from a godly woman who follows this God-inspired pattern:

Verses 10-12, 23 The husband/wife relationship
_____
_____

Verses 13-14 The stewardship of money
_____
_____

Verses 15, 18 Time management
_____
_____

Verses 16, 24 The use of talents and abilities
_____
_____

Verses 15, 19, 21-22, 27 Domestic chores
_____
_____

Verse 25 Attitude toward life
_____
_____
_____

Spiritual Dimensions

Verses 26, 28-29 Relationships
_____
_____

Verses 30-31 Relationship with God
_____
_____

GROWING, SHARING, SERVING

WOMEN'S LEADERSHIP FORUM

NAME _____
ADDRESS _____
_____

PHONE

Check areas of service you would be interested in serving, are now involved, or would attend a follow-up meeting to receive more information. Put "A" in the ☐ if you would serve in an administrative, organizational capacity, "S" if you want to help implement the program in a practical way by offering your time and service, or an "I" if you are already involved. Check as many as you wish.

PERSON-TO-PERSON

☐ Little Sister Program
☐ Mother-Daughter Workshops
☐ Counseling (problem areas)
☐ Singles
☐ Widows
☐ Discipleship

Spiritual Dimensions

PRACTICAL MINISTRIES

☐ Practical Arts ☐ Diet, Health, Exercise, First Aid
☐ Personal Development ☐ Preschool Observation
☐ Practicalities of Motherhood and Child Raising

SERVICE MINISTRIES

☐ Deaconess ☐ Helps
☐ Nursery ☐ Tutoring
☐ Baby Sitter Service

EVANGELISM AND OUTREACH

☐ Women For Missions ☐ Feminars
☐ Retreats ☐ Evangelism
☐ Juvenile Hall ☐ Hospital Service

GROWING, SHARING, SERVING

SPIRITUAL DIMENSIONS

☐ Prayer Hotline ☐ Scriptural Resource Library
☐ Leaders' Discipleship/Program Coordinators
☐ Bible Teachers ☐ Teaching Children (age 3—grade 6)

Please let us know of any other needs:

_____
_____
_____

Do you have any suggestions or comments?

_____
_____
_____

Meetings that will involve further discussion of your service in the area in which the Lord leads will be held on the following dates:

Monday, Dec. 6, 7:30 P.M.—Person-to-Person
Tuesday, Dec. 7, 7:30 P.M.—Practical Ministries
Tuesday, Dec. 7, 7:30 P.M.—Service Ministries
Wednesday, Dec. 8, 7:30 P.M.—Evangelism and Outreach
Thursday, Dec. 9, 7:30 P.M.—Spiritual Dimensions

Please note these dates on your calendar. You will receive a reminder in the mail within the next two weeks stating where your meeting will be held.